The Liberated
A new leadership para
Personal Share Price method

By
Stuart Drew

PublishNation

www.publishnation.co.uk

Professor Julian Birkinshaw, London Business School

"This is a terrific book. Stuart Drew offers a fresh and insightful look at the world of management, through anecdotes from his own highly-successful career. At its heart, the book is about taking control of your own destiny: your own "Personal Share Price" or PSP is an indicator of how much you are valued by those around you, and Stuart shows how you can build your PSP, to the benefit of your employees, your bosses, and yourself."

Vineet Nayar, past CEO HCL Technologies and Founder Chairman of Sampark Foundation. Author of the critically acclaimed book 'Employee First- Customer Second: Turning Conventional Management Upside Down' (Harvard Business Press) that sold over 100,000 copies

'Stuart, you led a team that fearlessly paved many new trails that others were quick to follow... you have always run ahead and shown the way... you built a spirit of experimentation in your team, where darkness means excitement, uncertainty means hope and risk is seen as an opportunity. Most importantly you led a team that had a big heart. The big heart makes it a caring place where people don't just want to work at but rather belong to. You have been a wonderful co-traveller and fellow dreamer.....in our fantastic transformation. This

learning captured in your book will be of great value to others'.

Patti Stevens, MSc
Founder, Association for Professional Executive Coaching & Supervision (APECS)

'Managers and their teams are at the heart and soul of every company. The coaching and mentoring of these people, new to management, or longer standing, is vital to the success of the business. Insights and techniques learned and honed by Stuart through his own deep corporate and personal experience are clearly and engagingly explained in this very readable book. It provides an indispensable resource for coaching managers through frameworks, models and thinking like Personal Share Price that liberates them from traditional burdens, thereby achieving differentiated performance with impressive business results'.

Anand Pillai, Managing Director Leadership Matters

'There are plenty of books out there with so called "practical" management tips written from a very universal perspective. What I find different in Stuart's book – 'How to Become a Liberated Manager' is that the he shares his life's rich experiences in practical nuggets that can be applied by us who are working in the corporate world. Stuart has packaged these practical

lessons, in wonderful, easy to remember models. The Book brings out the concept of 'Personal Share Price' in a very compelling manner. In addition Stuart explains through relevant examples, how to deliver outstanding sales performance from proposals through his D.I.D - Differentiated, Innovative and Disruptive approach. Throughout the book there are powerful elements that are associated with how to empower, enthuse and encourage teams to perform beyond their expectations while overcoming fears and assumed limitations of the manager. 'How to Become a Liberated Manager' is a must-read for all who need help in getting prepared to tackle the myriad challenges of managing people in today's agile world'.

Contents

Introduction

Are you concerned about being valued as a manager? Do you feel the need to 'have all the answers'? Do you worry too much about work? Are some of your peers doing better than you? Have you hired some people you wish you hadn't? Are you at ease with the global, multi-cultural world? Are you still relevant in this fast-changing world? Is your thinking tethered to what has worked in the past? If any of these questions make you feel uncomfortable by evoking a 'yes', then the good news is that you are not alone. The better news is that as the author of this book, I have been there, done that, and got the T-shirt. The T-shirt reads 'I am a liberated manager.'

I wish to share the delight and well-being in becoming a liberated manager. I contend that the course for graduation of becoming a liberated manager is open to all of us and is much more straightforward than might be imagined.

These pages will explore, through personal experience, how I became a liberated manager and the joy I feel upon witnessing other managers rise to become better than they think they are. That, I believe, is the potential for everyone. Crucially, in the first chapter, I introduce the concept of a Personal Share Price (PSP) that managers should understand and nurture. Once appreciated, managing one's PSP is the route to sustained liberation and fulfilment. It is also a way of controlling your own destiny through increased self-awareness. The formal process to measure a manager's performance in a company through annual appraisals is a lagging indicator of value. By contrast, awareness of one's

Personal Share Price as a means of self-government is intended more as a leading indicator of value and prospects.

In my career, I have worked for some excellent companies that are leaders in their fields. I have also witnessed the unpleasant and cancerous elements of business politics, something that I am ashamed to say I became competent at, but preferred to avoid. I have worked in global IT services and financial services, and I have been a non-executive director of a quoted global software company. I have also worked for a so-called 'big 4' global consulting firm as well as a dot-com startup. I was a European board member for a global insurance trade association and the chairman of a private members club. My most recent role was as an executive vice president at HCL Technologies Ltd (HCL), an India-based, global provider of IT services. All of these experiences contributed to my liberation as a manager. However, it was at HCL that I finally reached the pinnacle as a liberated manager by maximising my Personal Share Price. Prior to that, I had an extensive period of experience-based development on personal liberation within management, which the following chapters cover.

Over the last several years, I have been fortunate to work with and lead teams across the world in the IT service sector. These teams have delivered $500 million of annual revenue with an outstanding performance of over 30% compound annual growth rate (CAGR) over 12 years, which is twice the company average in revenue and profit. The teams have been multi-cultural and have not only enjoyed tremendous success but also, and more importantly, have had great comradeship. I have smiled through the last 15 years or more, and others have told me that I smile a lot.

People have asked me if there are any insights that I could share from my management experiences. The main observation that I could think of is that during my career, I developed into a liberated manager. This realisation was the motivation for me to write this book as I have too often encountered managers who do not smile a great deal and seem burdened with their role. If I can help them become more liberated, I believe that both their personal well-being and business performance will improve.

I have enjoyed a rewarding career while working for some stellar companies with wonderful people. During the many years that I spent working in IT and financial services, I have been through and orchestrated major change programmes and business transformations. These include a global transformation at HCL under the banner Employee First, the third largest merger in history to create Unisys and a complete revamp of the retail business at Prudential UK. I have worked with multi-cultural colleagues from whom I have learnt a great deal about compassion, humility, work ethic, determination and cultural difference. I have been lucky enough to have enjoyed a very successful career, and it has been a privilege to work with many colleagues, customers, and clients to create mutual value.

As a younger man, I was somewhat arrogant and self-centred, and I am sure that some who knew me then will recall that I was occasionally unpleasant to work with. However, enough people, including family, helped me become more proficient and rounded as a person.

Along the way, I have grown from only wanting to work with like-minded people to understanding that truly differentiated performance comes from working with a mix of individuals. I have also found that those different from myself can contribute disproportionately to my success.

I have gone from wanting exclusive success for myself to appreciating that well-managed teams perform better than individuals. I have learnt that a diversity of ideas makes us all wiser. I now appreciate the fact that real job satisfaction is in helping colleagues rise to become better than they think they are. Facilitating this growth of one's colleagues is the ultimate reward in management.

My journey to becoming a liberated manager was gradual. I arrived at the notion after several experiences and a realisation that as we progress as managers, our performance is increasingly dependent on others and less and less on ourselves. In this regard, creating an environment where teams are enthused, encouraged, and empowered to release their full potential is where liberation and smiles can be found. I offer my experiences as a potential shortcut for others or affirmation that they are on the right lines.

An important catalyst for my development as a liberated manager was participating in a major transformation at HCL. HCL enjoyed incredible growth and global recognition for a business transformation that began in 2005. The story became a Harvard Business School case study of a company growing from well under $600 million in annual revenue to more than $6.5 billion with market-leading growth in profit. This growth occured in just 11 years, three of which spanned The Great Recession that began in 2007. By 2014, HCL was among the eight fastest-growing global companies together with the likes of Amazon and Google.

The structure of this book covers various areas that contribute overall to liberating managers from traditional burdens like the perceived need to have all the answers for day-to-day issues and challenges. The book can be read as individual chapters or from start to finish, as each chapter tackles an independent but related topic on the path to liberation. There are several mentions of the transformation programme that I experienced at HCL, which was later called the Employee First Customer Second (EFCS) programme. However, the topics in the chapters are not limited to having a direct experience like EFCS. For me, the lessons are valid in all the environments that I have worked in: from command-and-control organisations to federated global consulting firms to companies weighed down by internal politics as well as empowered companies, one of which HCL became. At the end of each chapter, I have included liberation summaries as quick reference guides.

A new basis for measuring your value to business – Personal Share Price

As a manager, how do you measure your worth in a business context? This is a particularly relevant question for managers, as their performance invariably depends on the collective performance of their team(s). Sir Alex Ferguson and subsequent managers never played football for Manchester United but used their presence, behaviour, and experience to manage the Manchester United staff and players to achieve great heights for the club. In 2017, ManU, as they are affectionately known, became the most valuable football club in the world according to KPMG.

In the past, 'the numbers' were paramount in business. 'Did you achieve or exceed your agreed targets?' is a commonly asked question to judge performance. These measures shed no light on the 'how' of what you did and did not do, much less on the behaviours that you portrayed to others inside and outside the business. Some companies introduced annual appraisals as a way of casting some light on the 'how', but the business performance against objectives would overshadow any measures associated with things like employee engagement, empowerment, and team development.

Furthermore, a decade or so ago, business was much less dynamic than it is today. Companies could operate much more easily in uncontested markets. With increasing globalisation, the performance factors are far less predictable and are often influenced by external factors that are geopolitical. The financial market crisis, the China slowdown, and Brexit are examples of phenomena that affect companies' performance in ways that just cannot be forecast or negated. The challenge becomes one of an ability to react to events and thrive in the process.

With increasing market and political volatility, the traditional measures of management through target setting and three-year plans (they used to be five-year plans) are increasingly of less relevance to the actual outcomes. So, if a manager misses a performance target, uncontrollable external events frequently become the excuse. For example, a movement in currency exchange due to geopolitics can improve or impair revenue and profitability. Similarly, events like extreme weather, terrorist attacks, and electoral change, among others, impact performance but are increasingly unpredictable.

Nowadays, with the world 'connected' in so many ways and new business opportunities riding on the back of ever cheaper and more capable technology, we are witnessing a quantum shift in the way the world functions. This is changing the way business is done, the way we work, and the way we live. There is no longer an expectation or desire for what our parents or grandparents might have called a 'job for life'. This illusion, or even desire, disappeared a few years ago. The change is happening fast, and many traditional business models are now challenged by new, disruptive entrants. Tesla all-electric luxury cars are outselling the traditional global manufacturers in their class. Tesla launched their first car in 2008, and by 2017 became the most valuable car manufacturer in the world, as measured by market capitalisation. Tesla overtook the global giant General Motors that was established in 1908, one hundred years before Tesla shipped its first car. Tesla has no dealership arrangements and has a truly ground-breaking design philosophy for cars with zero emission, world-class acceleration, and a range in excess of 300 miles. Tesla advertises that their cars get smarter day by day unlike normal cars. This is because software updates are sent via the internet to add features like automatic parking and hands-free driving, a real example of the so-called Internet of Things (IOT) at a familiar, personal level. The Atom Bank in Britain recently received a banking licence. The bank has no branches, no ATM network, no cheque book, and an information-only website; it is entirely based on banking by mobile phone. Uber created a new way of hiring a taxi on a global basis and became a multi-billion dollar business. It began in 2009 and celebrated its fifth anniversary on June 1, 2015, with an announcement that it had grown into a transportation network spanning 311 cities in 58 countries. Airbnb was established in 2007 enabling people to lease or rent short term lodging. By 2017 Airbnb had three million lodging listings in 65,000 cities across 191 countries and has disrupted the global hospitality industry.

These quantum shifts are developing more quickly, and as managers and employees, we need to recognise what is happening and adapt to remain relevant. Remaining relevant is now, more than ever, a key skill that requires being open to learning and the challenges of the established ways of working.

In thinking about how I could measure my own value in an increasingly changing world, I conceived that the principal thing was what I called my 'Personal Share Price' (PSP). This is an abstract and volatile concept that is valued daily and is not linear with regard to performance. It is a result of interactions with colleagues, peers, superiors, customers, partners, team members, and even friends and family. It remains unpublished, but it can be measured through an honest appraisal of oneself. I chose the concept of a Personal Share Price as it seemed appropriately analogous to the workings of financial markets. A quoted company's share price provides a measure of valuation on a day-to-day basis. Furthermore, a share price is generally a leading indicator of future performance. By contrast, an employee's six-monthly or annual appraisal is mainly a lagging indicator of past performance only and provides little or no guide to the future.

Past performance alone is not the determinant of a corporate share price in financial markets. There are many examples in the corporate world of a share price falling against good reported performance and vice versa. Two high-profile examples validate the point. In July 2015, a headline in The Guardian newspaper in the UK read as follows: 'Apple stock continues to tumble despite better-than-expected earnings.' The article went on to say that 'investors had become accustomed to significant earnings beats by Apple.' Thus, the performance was good, but the expectation was even higher, and the shares fell. Similarly, companies can report relatively poor earnings, but the share price can rise. In February 2016, Royal Dutch Shell, the global oil company, reported that its full-year earnings fell by 53%, and yet, the share price rose by 7% on the news! I do not intend to rationalise the workings of stock markets, but a share price is influenced by, among other things, future expectations of business, dividend policy, Return on Investment (RoI), and market sentiment, and not just performance.

There is so much more to a share price than past performance alone. Therefore, I firmly believe that the same concepts should apply to managers in assessing their contribution and value in the workplace.

I contend that the Personal Share Price has three main components, namely behaviour, presence, and performance. These are further examined in this section. I believe that an appreciation and understanding of Personal Share Price is the first step on the road to liberation as a manager. I recall from my time at Unisys that an executive was called by a Human Resources (HR) representative to ask him why none of his staff had been given an appraisal for the last three years. His response was memorable, 'What do you mean? They get one every day!' He was clearly thinking in terms of a daily Personal Share Price.

To help illustrate the point further, imagine a few individuals whose presence, behaviour, and performance impact their standing or Personal Share Price. Richard Branson has managed to take the Virgin brand from music to airlines, to financial services, telecommunications, and even wedding stores and perfumery, the last two less than successful. However, many believe that Richard Branson has the Midas touch. Contrarily, Bernie Madoff, US stockbroker and financier, had the Midas touch for a while and then was revealed as a fraudster for which he was convicted and jailed. Warren Buffet is an American business magnate, investor, and philanthropist. He is considered by many to be one of the most successful investors in the world. Richard (Dick) Fuld was a chief executive officer, who, on September 15, 2008, led Lehman Brothers into the largest bankruptcy in US history. A few years earlier he had been hailed as a master of corporate growth. Just imagine how the Personal Share Price of these famous individuals faired over time. In the entertainment industry, singers and actors come and go, and sports stars rise and fall. Imagine the Personal Share Price over a number of years of O. J. Simpson, Marion Jones, David Beckham, Tom Jones, Robert Downey Jr, Adele, Amy Winehouse, Mike Tyson, and Tiger Woods, and you have the idea of Personal Share Price in extremis. It is also possible to imagine the extent to which their behaviour impacted their performance and presence and vice versa. In some of the examples, their presence remained intact, and in others, it did not. In some cases, they maintained their PSP after retirement upon moving into different fields, and in others, they pushed the self-destruct button. This provides some basis for imagining the volatility of PSP on a day-to-day basis.

Another simple way to imagine the concept of a Personal Share Price, is to consider how some of the business models like Airbnb, eBay, Amazon and Uber sustain success. They use collaboration feedback systems. In 1997, eBay introduced a feature called Seller Feedback. In any transaction the seller rates the buyer and the buyer rates the seller. The idea of both parties rating each other after a transaction has become ubiquitous in on-line trading platforms.

When you buy something online - you rate the seller and the seller rates you. When you hire a taxi service, like Uber - you rate the driver, the driver rates you. If you stay in an Airbnb registered property - you rate the host and the host rates you. After seeing a few positive reviews your mind is set at ease about an otherwise stranger. Imagine a similar but more complex system operating within a company among colleagues who work with each other as supplier and internal customer. More importantly subliminally external customers are rating suppliers all the time, sometimes revealed through an annual satisfaction survey but more often on experiences from day to day interactions.

These examples set the scene for comprehending the concept of a Personal Share Price (PSP) as a measure of successful leadership.

At a more down-to-earth level, people ask me if PSP is a thing that matters how can one know if it is in good shape. I reply as follows:

- People (customers, colleagues, and partners) will return your calls promptly;
- People will reply to your emails;
- People will seek your advice;
- People will want to join your team;
- People will want to work on your projects;
- People will want you to work on their projects;
- Seniors and peers will seek and value your opinion;
- You will never have a problem in getting to meet the people you want to meet;
- Your performance will be superior to your peers; and
- You will have assumed authority that is disproportionate to your job grade
- People will go the extra mile for you without being asked

This is by no means an exhaustive list, but it sets the tone for understanding the basics of PSP. These are some of the indicators of success in its wider sense. In other words, as a manager, it is people that make you successful, and successful people attract good people to want to work with them. In uncertain and changing times, I do believe that the concept of PSP is as good as any formal metric based on revenue, profit or growth and the like. These are acknowledged performance metrics that are important but not necessarily pre-eminent.

That being said, performance is clearly impactful on a share price. Performing consistently according to or better than the expectations will undoubtedly contribute to a healthy PSP. However, the aspects of behaviour and presence should not be subordinated to performance in doing the complete job, including developing and nurturing teams for sustained success. This applies in particular to managers, as their performance is generally an aggregation of their teams' performance. Thus, it can be argued that a manager's behaviour and presence, in fact, drives the performance of their team. Behaviour is a key driver of performance. It is important here to dismiss personality as a component of Personal Share Price. Definitive research by Walter Mischel, psychology professor while at Stanford University, found that personality explains less than 10% of a person's behaviour. Personality is a poor predictor of performance because people are highly adaptive and far more flexible than personality tests give them credit for. To emphasise the point, Professor Robin Stuart-Kotze wrote a book entitled 'Performance: The Secrets of Successful Behaviour', in which behaviour far outweighed any impact from personality in sustained success.

Similarly, developing personal presence (and it can be developed) is important for sustained achievement. We recognise personal presence in people who are confident, at ease, and true to themselves. They exude energy, are noticed, listened to, trusted, respected and followed. Personal presence is not about who is loudest or who has the biggest ego. Personal presence is a state of being that allows you to develop more choices, reduce fears, and influence those around you. People with presence also behave in a way that puts others at ease; they listen attentively and invite contributions without fear of reprimand or ridicule. They are measured in all that they do.

The notion of behaviour and presence being peers to performance became evident to me when, as a part of HCL's transformation under the EFCS strategy (more of which is discussed later), the company introduced 360° feedback for managers. The feedback system was online and involved a questionnaire for rating a manager across various desired behaviours. In my experience, most large companies perform this but do not publish the results on their intranet. In HCL, the 360° feedback had more to do with behaviour and presence than performance. The performance was measured separately through a different appraisal system. The 360° feedback in HCL has some unusual aspects. Of course, it sought feedback from superiors, peers, and subordinates (360°) from within the business unit, but it also included 'outsiders' to the line management function. The contributions from line management outsiders were called Happy Feet.

Happy Feet recognised that in today's complex businesses, teams are formed and disbanded for short periods to address specific projects or tasks, like producing a client proposal or addressing a particular business improvement issue. In any given year, people interact across departments and function on an ad-hoc or temporary basis. Happy Feet was designed for these casual interactions to be included in an individual's 360° behavioural review. Thus, seniors, peers, subordinates, and other occasional work colleagues formed the total 360° feedback process. As previously mentioned, the 360° feedback was presence and behaviour oriented. The questionnaire asked respondents to rate the individual on a scale of 1–5 for things, such as approachability, care in listening, assistance with finding solutions, encouraging freedom to act, tangible empowerment, cross function collaboration, and cooperation. These measures were important because the company wanted to empower decision making at all levels to release individual and team potential so as to deliver differentiated customer value. In essence, the 360° feedback could be seen as an annual report on one's PSP.

This came home to me in a very specific experience that I had with a fellow senior manager named Sullivan. I joined HCL in the UK at the same time as Sullivan joined in India. Sullivan was the delivery head for IT services to global insurance clients. He was an Indian Christian based in Chennai, and he had the responsibility for a staff contingent of around 2000 people. Over several years, we became close, as he was my offshore service delivery partner and a good friend. I had worked with Sullivan for many years and visited him in his office whenever I visited Chennai. One day I arrived unannounced at his office, he looked up and invited me with a hand gesture while sitting at his desk. I went in, and he did not look his usual cheerful self. I sat down, but I sensed that something was wrong. We exchanged greetings, but I could tell that he was preoccupied. I asked him why he looked so unhappy. He then recounted a story about how, due to his good performance, he had been given global banking delivery services in addition to his insurance franchise. This entailed delivering IT services to insurance and banking clients across the globe. He then said that he had recently been asked to take on the capital markets' IT delivery as well, which, in total, would have included responsibility for an IT workforce of some 9000 people. 'So why unhappy?' I asked. He then said that despite this increase in responsibility, he had not received the pay rise that he felt was commensurate and had not been promoted in that year. What was worse in his eyes was the fact that several colleagues whom he considered his peers had been promoted, so he was fed up. I asked him if he had taken this up with his reporting manager or even the CEO. He said that he had and the response was that he had not been promoted because his 360° feedback 'had not shown momentum' over the past three years. In other words, *what* he was doing was fine, but *how* he was doing it was not supportive of enthusing, encouraging, and empowering his colleagues. He was a command-and-control manager, who could not adjust to a more liberalised way of working. In fact, the previous year he was given the same feedback on his behaviour, but he had not implemented tangible actions to change. Needless to say, Sullivan left the organisation a few months later.

For me, this was a powerful example of how someone could be seen as performing well and increasing their scope of work but adversely impacting their PSP. I also found the phrase 'had not shown momentum' very powerful. It was an indication that people were not expected to change behaviours overnight, but they should show some momentum towards the desired behaviours with a new business strategy. As a result of this experience, I ask myself if I show momentum towards the desired behaviours that are required by an ever-changing world with a new breed of the social media–savvy workforce and customers. Hierarchy is, in many places, being replaced with a more democratic work environment. Are we showing a momentum towards this ever-changing world? The Roman Catholic Cardinal Newman put it well when he said, 'to live is to change; to live well is to change often'. The Roman Catholic Church is hardly the benchmark for significant change, but it clearly is sensitive to change around it. The response to change in each of us will positively or negatively impact our PSP.

In any given marketplace, there are analysts and industry commentators that support and promote a company, and hence, talk up the share price. However, the opposite is also applicable. Some detractors have a more negative view on a given company, and in the worst case, they become publicly hostile and depress the share price.

Similarly, as careers develop, it is inevitable that you will create supporters as well as detractors or enemies. This could be for a number of reasons. Some people will resent your success, some will be jealous of your ability to get along with others, some will want your job and be happy to undermine you, and I am sure there are many other reasons. The point is that you can do nothing about other people and can only influence them by your own behaviour and presence. To prosper in various corporate environments, it is important that you are alive to potential enemies but behave in a way that minimises their impact on you.

In the year 2000, in addition to my work, I was elected as the chairman of a private members' club with around 3000 members. There were all shades of folk, members were mostly over 40 years of age, and many had retired from successful careers in business. In such a club, there were people with opinions on everything, such as how things should be done, what is not right, why things aren't working properly – mature complainers. There were also well-wishers and supporters of the governing body that was called the Council. In fact, the club was a registered company, and the chairman (myself) held the majority of shares. When the club underwent a period of change, there was a cadre of members who wanted to replace the Council with like-minded folk to resist the change. It was through this experience that I arrived at a realisation that has served me well ever since. The notion was to assume that 25% of members will love you whatever you do, and 25% will hate you whatever you do. Thus, the trick is to worry about the 50% in the middle! In the event, a special meeting was held, and the majority of the club members supported the existing Council. Thus, I learnt that focusing on the 50% would ultimately determine my Personal Share Price as the chairman. Spending time on the 25% who were detractors was a waste of effort and best ignored, and nurturing the 25% who were well-wishers paid handsome dividends. I imagine that many politicians work on a similar principle.

Through working in different organisations across a spectrum of those rife with internal politics to enlightened businesses where openness and transparency prevail, I have learnt a great deal. Some techniques that helped me, then and since, to protect and enhance my Personal Share Price are as follows:

The first lesson came when I was at Unisys, hosting a public sector client executive conference in St. Paul de Vence in France. Due to the prestigious location, it was not difficult to attract willing board-level delegates and their partners to attend the annual conference. In turn, the quality of delegates made it easier to attract prominent speakers that were leaders in their fields. Each year, among the invited speakers, I invited two Members of Parliament – one from the government in power and one from the opposition benches. The conference typically lasted three days with an appropriate agenda and significant time for relaxation and networking. As partners were invited, there was a parallel agenda for them while the business sessions were in progress.

In this closed environment, the MPs and their partners interacted with delegates and were invariably warm hearted. Indeed, the MPs were cheerful, and they bantered light-heartedly with one another. This was observed by the delegates and their partners, and they frequently asked why the MPs were not similarly convivial on television or radio broadcasts. How do MPs who disagree so profoundly on political issues become 'mates' and personal friends outside the House of Commons?

I noticed two things that help explain this and have helped me since in my day-to-day business dealings.

The first is that in Parliament, all comments and questions are addressed to the Speaker or the chairman of proceedings. None is addressed to crossbench individuals. Secondly, when referring to individuals on the other side of the house, they are addressed as the right honourable member for their constituency. This may seem like pomp and circumstance, but it has very practical benefits. No one can be personally or directly offended!

The point from these observations is that in the political interactions, criticism, sometimes vehement criticism, is made of the idea, proposal, or policy under debate but not the person.

I learnt that this philosophy was invaluable in business. I can challenge anyone's proposal, viewpoint, or idea without the need to criticise the individuals themselves. Thus, in conversation, it is important to distinguish the point being made by the individual making it. In this way, mutual respect can prevail. I have seen the opposite too many times when an idea, proposal, or viewpoint is personalised with comments such as the following: 'he doesn't know what he is talking about', 'she is just plain crazy', 'he is off his rocker', and the like, all of which are deeply personal and deeply offensive.

Thus, to maintain or enhance your PSP, remember to critique ideas, proposals, policies, and viewpoints but not the individual making them.

Another thing I learnt is blatantly obvious but strangely rare in business, which is never to lie to yourself or others and never to guess an answer. It amazes me how many people are tempted to lie or guess rather than accept a shortcoming of knowledge. Integrity should be regarded much like virginity; you can only lose it once! Too often, a lie in a business context manifests itself from the point of not having the facts. The lie can then often be disguised as a guess. But even an informed guess is a lie, is it not? The Dictionary.com definition of a lie is as follows: 'a false statement deliberately presented as being true'. The same dictionary's definition of a guess is 'to conclude something without sufficient information of being correct'. 'True' and 'correct' are quite similar, are they not?

The strange point is that we should all expect that a guessed response to a question that we do not know the answer to will be exposed. I have seen some terrible responses to questions during a senior management review; we used to call them 'car-crash answers' to questions like 'what share of wallet does the customer have with our firm?', 'what is their annual turnover and how is that split across their businesses?', and 'which companies are their major competitors?' These questions have the potential to damage one's PSP severely, and persistence with an incorrect or guessed answer may end up in the shares being suspended!

Instead, the proper response should be 'I don't know but will find out. How quickly do you want the answer?' A note of caution here: there are many things that a manager should know in order to be effective. Shortcomings regarding required knowledge elements will quite rightly be an issue about competence and adversely impact PSP. However, when there are questions that you do not know the answer to, admit it. On the occasions, which are hopefully rare, when guessing gets the better of you, check the facts and revert to the questioner, 'Remember you asked me that question and I said X, I was wrong, I have checked and it is in fact Y.'

All human beings make mistakes but do not declare them too often, in the mistaken belief that it hasn't been spotted. My advice is always to assume that it will be detected sooner or later. Rectifying the error and admitting it will help to maintain your PSP and may even enhance it.

Some simple things can be done to improve your PSP through your behaviour. Just like in a company, the marketing message and 'appearance' of the enterprise can send strong messages. I once worked for a company that spent £500k on changing its logo. Nothing other than the logo changed, as the previous logo had been associated with being 'old fashioned'. The company wanted to attract a younger customer base, and a new logo was the answer! In another case, while at Prudential Corporation, a new retail bank was launched to harbour insurance maturity deposits. Insurance is, by nature, a somewhat boring industry. In fact, we used to say that boring was good. It sent messages of stability, solidity, and deep and profound foundations that had stood the test of time and were, in effect, the antitheses of what qualifies as exciting and risk taking. However, a new bank in the internet era would likely not benefit from such a message or appearance. A PR company was hired to come up with some ideas, and suggested a shortlist of new bank names Oxygen, 360, and Egg. After deliberation we chose Egg. Egg was launched and became very successful, but few knew that the traditional firm

Prudential was the parent company. The Prudential share price rose as Egg had a successful launch and simultaneously demonstrated the organisation's more modern outlook.

Similarly, as people, we need to promote our image and appearance to enhance our PSP. I will call this aspect of PSP your presence or gravitas. Presence has been defined earlier but is evident in all strong managers and leaders. In summary, it is the combination of integrity, confidence, self-belief, strong body language, social interaction, and sense of humour. Many people think that presence cannot be developed and is innate, but that is not true. Presence can be developed. Dianna Booher authored a book in 2011 entitled *Creating Personal Presence*. The book includes a self-assessment for personal presence. Jo Ousten & Co is a career development company that specialises in developing presence. Their strap line is 'we all come into the world with presence but so often we lose it'. Developing personal presence is therefore critical to an improved and sustained PSP. For example, people like working with people that have a confident smile. It sends a message of comfort with oneself, and an openness to be approached – simple but true. Just think of the opposite. If you see a stern-looking person, you are much more likely to keep your distance. Similarly, look smart in your clothes and appearance. Avoid the temptation to be dandy or dishevelled as the two extremes. Being smart is associated with a professional demeanour, rightly or wrongly.

Thank people who work with you and for you. This is such a simple statement, but it is very powerful. I recall an experience that I had with a secondary school head teacher. The term 'head teacher' was largely a misnomer, as the head of a large school spends little time teaching! Instead, they are, in fact, running a small business with a need to understand budgeting, HR, forecasting, customer interaction with pupils and parents, and many other skills that are more familiar to a business leader. In the UK, when this was recognised, the government introduced a programme for business leaders to volunteer to coach and mentor local head teachers. The programme was called 'Partners in Leadership'. I became a steering committee member for the national programme and participated as a coach and mentor to a local head teacher. When I first met Mr Turnbull, who was the head teacher of a local secondary school with several hundred pupils, he was somewhat suspicious of the programme and curious as to whether I was, in fact, a spy of some sort. Soon, I dispelled his fears and told him that I was only there to help him if he needed it and that all our conversations were private and there would be no record of our meetings. When he relaxed, I asked him about his challenges and the things he would like to improve. We worked on a few items that had concerned him, for which my business experience had relevance, and we discussed actions that he could implement to improve or address his challenges. However, when I got to know him better, he eventually said that one of his biggest concerns was that he felt that his staff did not like him and considered him aloof and remote. We talked for some time, and from the information he gave me, I asked him how often he thanked his team members. He choked on a laugh and then said that he did not thank his staff for doing their jobs. I then asked him if any of his staff took on extra duties during the school day or after school. He began reeling off a number of staff members who had taken on additional responsibilities without rewards. I then said, 'and you have never thanked them?' He confirmed that he felt uncomfortable doing so. I then told him that in my business I had made some postcards with 'Thank You' printed on the front and a blank reverse. I would hand write these cards to people who deserved a 'thank you' and leave it on their desk or in their pigeonhole. I had done this for several years and told him that some people pinned the note up on their workstation, and it remained there for ages. Others kept them or took them home. Very few ended up in the bin! I asked him if he would consider doing the same. He agreed, and I offered to meet with the staff who had received a 'thank you' note to see how it had been received. After a couple of months, I met some staff and they said that in the beginning, they thought it was a joke as it was contrary to Mr Turnbull's previous behaviour. However, as each note had a specific reference to a particular person, they soon began to appreciate the notes and value them. This small gesture had a disproportionate impact in bringing staff and the head teacher closer together through a realisation that contributions had indeed been recognised before the postcards began but were not exhibited. Mr Turnbull's personal presence improved as he was deemed more approachable.

In my own business, I make it a point to thank people who have done something extra verbally, and when it is something beyond the normal expectations, I send a 'Thank You' note as mentioned above. In HCL, I insisted on thanking the offshore delivery teams for their contributions in providing customers with exceptional service. In the board-level reviews, I would specifically refer to where the delivery team had exceeded expectations. This was appreciated by the heads of the delivery. By contrast, a peer of mine would invariably criticise the delivery teams for failing to fulfil up to 100% of the customer opportunities presented. This would frequently end in an argument with no conclusion. I generally sat back, smiled, and was not at all surprised that the service to my business unit was superior! Showing genuine appreciation for people's efforts is always rewarding and improves the PSP. Similarly, knowing something personal about the people you work with is as important as it is in your personal life. Remembering birthdays and job anniversaries is simple and appreciated. HR has the details, and all you have to do is send a personal email acknowledging the event with a suitable message. Other important life events for team members are also well worth recognition – weddings, births, and even vacations. This should not be a burden but a regular behaviour. People remember it for years when a CEO recognises an individual as a person rather than an employee. Managers should be no different. I was once introduced to Her Majesty Queen Elizabeth II when I was on the board of the private members club mentioned earlier. I am sure that she has not remembered me, but our picture remains on my wall forever.

The final part of presence as a support for PSP is maintaining a sense of humour. Business is a hectic pursuit in today's markets. Employees frequently work long and unsocial hours to get the job done. This can lead to stress in the workplace and worse if health becomes affected. It is an increasingly competitive world for business that brings with it increased personal stress. Interactions can become heated as teams strive to do their best, and on occasion, managers can grow intolerant of others' efforts. Tempers can fly as calm reasoning goes out of the window, and a destructive virus can take hold. One antidote to this virus is a sense of humour. I contend that a sense of humour ranks equally with strategic thinking and communication skills in a manager's presence. Dwight D Eisenhower said, 'a sense of humour is part of the art of leadership, of getting along with people, with getting things done'. A Robert Half International survey found that 91% of executives believe that a sense of humour is important for career advancement and 84% believe that people with a good sense of humour do a better job. One cautionary note is that a good sense of humour excludes cynicism or sarcasm, both of which are corrosive. Harvard Business Review published a paper by Alison Beard in May 2014 entitled 'Leading with Humour.' The opening paragraph read, 'The workplace needs laughter. According to research from institutions as serious as Wharton Business School, MIT, and London Business School, every chuckle or guffaw brings with it a host of business benefits. Laughter relieves stress and boredom, boosts engagement and well-being, and spurs not only creativity and collaboration but also analytic precision and productivity'. Somewhat depressingly, the article reported that we laugh significantly less on weekdays as we do on weekends and concluded that 'work is a sober endeavour'. So, developing a sense of humour, laughing at yourself, and a chortle show other people that things are okay. Laughing is disarming and best used to poke fun at things that everyone is worried about. Interestingly, although august voices, like those mentioned, talk of the value of a sense of humour in business, I have never a seen an appraisal system that includes it.

A final thought on PSP

I have been asked if the principles of Personal Share Price apply in traditional or oppressive companies. The short answer is yes, it does. I have worked, as stated earlier, in a company where corporate politics was rife. Managers would backstab each other and the management transparency was poor, so rumours were ever present. I heard numerous cases where staff members could remember the date that their careers halted when they had asked a senior manager a question they did not like. The company was unionised and the cause of much frustration was that the union had more control over its members than the company had over its staff – the very same people. One case that I recall is when I visited a branch office in Haverfordwest, a town in Wales. I arrived and was greeted by the branch manager. I had recently joined the company as a regional director and was touring the branches to introduce myself and share the region's objectives and plans for the coming year. The sessions normally ended with an open forum for questions from the staff. On this occasion, the branch staff were gathered in a training room. Upon entering the room, I noticed that there was no hubbub and the faces were stern. The branch manager introduced me. I thanked him and greeted the assembled team, with no response from them. I then covered the agenda for the meeting and presented the details. During the 45 minutes, there was not a sound or a smile. At the end, I asked if there were any questions and was met with stony silence. I persisted for a while, but nothing returned. The branch manager then closed the meeting, and we returned to his office. I asked him 'what was that all about?' He apologised but said that the union had got news of my visit. They were suspicious as I was the first manager of my rank to visit the branch in over 10 years! They had therefore assumed I had come to close the branch. In response, the union had told the branch staff to say nothing, do nothing, and wait for me to leave. I had a similar experience in a few more branches.

However, things improved as no branch closures were announced. A few months later, I returned to the branches where the reception had been most frosty and conducted a flip chart session asking the staff what was preventing further success. The details of such a session are covered in the chapter entitled Liberation from worrying too much and negativity. Suffice it to say that it established a rapport and the beginnings of trust between us. My PSP had gone from rock bottom as measured by the staff to improving much over the period. Over the next few months, many of the techniques for liberation covered in this book were implemented. When I left the company about 7 years later, the Welsh branches gave me the best send off I could imagine. They presented me with a caricature maquette of me in tennis gear and gave my wife a daffodil made of rare welsh gold (the daffodil is the national flower of Wales). My PSP had indeed risen. From a performance perspective, the region had outperformed the other regions for 5 of the 7 years that I was the regional director.

When I first joined HCL in the UK, I soon realised it was an oppressive environment. My introduction was a baptism of fire. I was appointed by the board in India to boost the level of the local senior managers in Europe. The board wanted new blood from outside their company, and I was headhunted from Deloitte Consulting. I was the fourth non-Indian to join HCL. I was asked to set up a new business team for large deals in the IT services sector. I duly joined to discover that the local management did not know I was arriving, and that my role was senior to all but one of the local managers. This was my first experience of being totally excluded. On the first day, I arrived and was guided to my office by the office manager. An hour later, the most senior manager in the office, Roger, walked in and introduced himself and asked what my brief was. After I told him, he said that he had the responsibility for what I was hired to do and that therefore I should report to him. However, my job offer stated my boss was in the USA. We agreed to differ. For the next few weeks, I was ignored. I was not invited to any internal meetings, and no one asked for my help or offered any help. To invite goodwill, I heard that the local team were looking to acquire a new customer where I knew the finance director well. I let the senior manager know, and he thanked me but said they could handle the deal without my help. My USA boss could not do much as he was also a new hire from Accenture and had not yet got to know the company. A few weeks passed, during which I had begun to speak to other people in the office and initiated the process of interviewing to recruit my new team. People began to sense my presence as I had much experience from large companies, a startup, and a global consulting firm. Our office chats would invariably result in me being perceived as 'not a bad chap' and someone who had the relevant experience that they lacked. My behaviour to my colleagues was balanced; I was just curious about why a company would employ someone of my experience if not to make a difference. Due to my unpleasant early experience, I began to contemplate if I should stay or resign. After two months, I was due to take a pre-planned holiday. Before I left, I asked to meet Roger; I told him I was due on holiday and that while I was away, I would be grateful if he would consider how we should work together to provide mutual value to the company that employed us both. I suggested that I could help with some of the deals that his team was working on, given my experience. He listened and said he would think about it but I left without expecting a change of heart.

When I returned from the holiday, I was amazed at what happened. Roger asked to see me urgently. He told me that they were on a huge deal (that I had known about) and that they thought they were in the lead to secure the contract. However, during a presentation that took place while I was on holiday, the client had told Roger that they were fourth out of four! When this news got to the head office, they immediately asked for me to take over the deal. Over the next few weeks, I managed the deal and brought in some new team members. Two months later, following the final competitive presentation, we were awarded the contract. From that day onwards, Roger referred to me as 'doctor Drew'! We became good friends soon afterwards. In essence, my PSP was revalued. It took time for the opportunity to add performance (winning the large deal) to my presence and behaviour. Following the large deal win, my portfolio changed to a wider brief and Roger moved on to a new assignment. A year later, the transformation of HCL began under the leadership of Vineet Nayar. In the following years, I implemented the ideas and techniques that are covered in this book. As a mark of my improved PSP, I was promoted to the position of senior vice president and then executive vice president, and Vineet wrote the kind words that endorse this book.

This section has covered the concept of PSP as a currency that values an individual manager's contribution in business. It has three main components: performance, behaviour, and presence. These can be considered with equal weighting, with behaviour being the first among equals.

In short, therefore, rather than the pay, performance, and job grade being the gold standard in career development, consider the concept of PSP, whether or not your company recognises the notion. Most companies use lagging indicators to measure a manager's performance; PSP is conceived more as a leading indicator. When people enquire about the opportunities for development in my company, I always say, 'be in control of your own destiny'. If you are aware of your PSP formally, like the 360° feedback or your own developed survey, or less formally, by how people react and respond to you, then you are in control. I always told the candidates at interviews that the only thing that mattered was one's PSP. It was a powerful way of conveying the importance of behaviour, performance, and presence as meaningful measures for sustained success. PSP also provides a solid foundation for liberation as a manager, as elaborated in the subsequent chapters.

Liberation summary:

- Understand that behaviour, performance, and presence are equal allies for your management development. Develop ways of measuring your PSP and reflect on it from time to time.
- Be genuinely open and honest at all times – think about how your imagined annual behavioural audit might look.
- Be transparent in your dealings with others, thus liberating yourself from a defensive mindset.

- Offer to help others, even when not asked and even if it has no benefit for you. Assume that there will be a time in the future when it will pay off.
- Seek feedback from people outside your team that you collaborate with from time to time. Ask them to rate you and your team and what improvements they would like to see. Consider developing your own PSP survey.
- Recognise the need to remain relevant in a fast-changing world, and take action to understand what developments are happening with younger people.
- Understand that you need to show momentum towards desired behaviours. These will be in addition to management basic behaviours, like doing what you say you will do and on time attendance at meetings.
- Don't criticise individuals but rather the ideas, proposals, and opinions that you do not agree with.
- Never lie and do not be tempted to guess.
- 'I don't know but will find out' is a perfectly acceptable response to questions that you do not know the answer to.
- Success in achieving your goals is a magnet for other high performers and enhances your PSP.
- Consider how you can improve your personal presence.
- Maintain a sense of humour, thank people formally, and take an interest in their personal lives.
- The principles of PSP work in all corporate environments because it depends on you.

Liberation from having to have all the answers

One of the pressures that manager put on themselves is the perceived need to 'have the answers' to their subordinates' issues, problems, and performance shortfalls. I fell into this trap in my early years in management. I felt that my power came from being ahead of my peers and team members in knowing what to do in various situations. I felt that I needed to be the 'go-to' man. I spent a disproportionate amount of time trying to gather as much information as possible, and it even got to the stage where my power could be protected by not sharing information. This I thought provided an additional magnet to attract the people seeking advice. I could not have been more wrong. It is foolhardy to assume that anyone has all the answers. When the availability of information on the worldwide web and company intranets is considered, there is more easily available information than any one person can consume.

I finally realised that supposedly having the answers also laid the ownership for solutions at my door. And that in itself is burdensome and the stuff of sleepless nights. Once I realised that I should facilitate finding solutions to problems and invite others to own the solution, I became liberated and, to somewhat to my surprise, more valued as a manager. I had in fact improved my presence, and my peers and colleagues valued my behaviour more. Strange but true. As I developed the skills of listening and empowering others, my team's performance, and thus my performance, improved. Here is a story that describes a case in point.

Brian came into my room, the door was open, and he asked me if I had a minute. I said that I had and invited him to sit down. You can tell when someone needs to speak. He began by venting his frustration at the existing bid management process we used to assess – whether to bid for a project or not.

We worked in the IT services business, where potential customers invite a number of companies to tender for large, multi-million dollar projects. The bid process would typically last a few months and the cost of bidding, in terms of time, effort, and money, was significant. Thus, most IT companies require a bid template to be completed and signed off before agreeing to submit a bid. The essence of the bid process is to determine the likelihood of winning.

Brian said that our process was deeply flawed, required too much irrelevant information, was cumbersome, and worst of all, was subject to manipulation of the answer. In other words, the bid or no-bid decision could be contrived.

I listened attentively. After several minutes of his passionate diatribe, he paused and said, 'I've just done it, haven't I?' I asked 'done what?' 'Volunteered', he replied. At that moment, I reached the pinnacle as a liberated manager. I said nothing, listened attentively, let Brian vent his frustration, and waited for him to realise that he was going to be the architect of his own solution.

This experience was in marked contrast to my early days as a manager, when I felt the need to have all the answers to the challenges that my team faced. I was ever eager to show them that I could help partly as a means of justifying my position. I had gone through various management training courses, but nothing prepares you for real life. I soon began to discern that I was accepting more and more responsibility for my team's success and the anxiety that went with it. Thankfully, I started to realise that my role was more to develop my team's capability to solve their problems rather than provide the solution for which I had total accountability and they had none! 'Well, it was your idea boss', these words or similar ones are a bad sign for managers. I have worked for CEOs who gave me extensive freedom to act, which was very rewarding and fulfilling but daunting at the same time. I have also worked for CEOs who have had all the answers, and I had the least job satisfaction, but I slept well! 'It was your idea, boss!'

I will continue this section with reference at length to a business transformation that I witnessed at close quarters. It may seem like a long digression, but it is important to understand the full context of the liberation that I experienced as a manager by enthusing, empowering, and encouraging people to deliver differentiated customer value. Through this experience, I learnt to devolve implementing solutions to most of my team's issues to my team members themselves. The team's performance rocketed, and my liberation flourished.

I was blessed to be part of a management and organisational revolution at HCL that was groundbreaking and global in its recognition. A new CEO was appointed in 2005 from within HCL. Vineet Nayar was truly a remarkable man who soon introduced the concept of EFCS that became a Harvard Business School and London Business School case study on business transformation. For those who have not read the book *Employee First – Customer Second*, I recommend reading it, and I offer some of my own experiences from being there at the beginning, during its evolution to the publication of the book and beyond.

HCL is today a $6.7 billion global IT Services company, with over 100,000 employees in 32 countries, based in India and headquartered in Delhi. In 2005, HCL reported annual revenues of $568 million and a rise in staff to 16,000. It was the year that Vineet Nayar was appointed as the new CEO. A few months after taking office, Vineet convened a meeting of the top 200 managers in the global business to which I was invited. The business meeting was called Blueprint. From this meeting, it emerged that Vineet was keen to solicit ideas and critique from the assembled global senior managers. The meeting naturally included an analysis of HCL's strengths, weaknesses, opportunities, and threats (SWOT). At that time, HCL was growing but not as fast as its major Indian Offshore Provider (IOP) competitors. During Blueprint, there were open forums on what we needed to correct, keep, and introduce. A proposition review and a filling of the gaps in the skills portfolio were called for. The meeting would have been recognisable to hundreds of companies worldwide.

But out of it came a remarkable insight that was the answer to a very simple question – what does HCL exist to do? As a global IT services company, the answer was as straightforward as the question. The answer was: to deliver differentiated customer value.

Simple so far. The next question – who in our organisation delivered value to our customers? Remembering that HCL was an IT services company and not a product company, the answer was as follows: Those HCL employees ('HCLites', we came to call ourselves) that worked directly with customers at their premises or from offshore geographic locations.

The platform was set – the site where HCLites worked directly with customers was where value was created. We called this the Value Zone. From this reality, there was an obvious conclusion that if the Value Zone was where the customer value is created, then *differentiated* customer value would most likely materialise if those HCLites working with customers were encouraged to release their full potential. By using their work experience and knowledge, they would be able to suggest value-added ideas to customers in order to create value beyond the contracted deliverables.

As an example, which will be elaborated later, developing an application for a customer would constitute a Statement of Work (SOW) or contract. Delivering the work within time and budget would represent what was required under the contract. However, the knowledge of the application interfaces that are necessary to complete the work would provide the opportunity to suggest other improvements like reducing the number of interfaces. Reducing the interfaces would likely make the system more efficient and less heavy on computing resources. If this could be quantified, then suggesting such changes would provide tangible, quantified value in excess of the contracted work. This would be an example of differentiated customer value.

However, if differentiated customer value comes from the people who work with customers, the next question was:

What is the role of the management? The conclusion was that the management's role was to enthuse, encourage, and empower the HCLites working with customers to deliver differentiated value. Eventually, we called the people who worked directly with customers the Value Creators.

An early obstacle was that changing from more of a command-and-control hierarchy that had existed for years to one with empowered employees required the employees to believe that it was real. Would my manager really change? What happens when I make a mistake? What if it doesn't last? What does it mean to be empowered? How can I deliver extra value? It may work in India, but what about other countries and cultures? These were some of the questions that we heard the employees asking.

To convince the employees that the senior management was serious about empowerment, the employees would have to trust them. But trust is the ultimate intangible. You cannot measure it; it is absolute and binary. I trust you or I don't. You cannot introduce an index for trust; you cannot incentivise trust or have a Key Performance Parameter (KPP) for trust. And yet, the power in the differentiated customer value proposition depended on the customer-facing employees believing that they were indeed empowered and encouraged to deliver differentiated customer value.

The idea was hatched that employee trust might be invited by 'pushing the envelope of transparency'. If the management shared information more openly and invited public critique, then employees would perhaps trust the rhetoric. A number of initiatives were then implemented. Among them was the launch of 360° feedback, an annual personal review system completed by superiors, peers, subordinates, and others, already referred to in the previous chapter. Many companies that I have dealt with had done this before HCL, but not one that I could ever find published the results of managers, up to and including the CEO, on their intranet for all their employees to see. This would have demonstrated true openness and transparency. HCL did, in fact, publish the results on the corporate intranet for all to see. 360° feedback was less to do with performance and more to do with behaviours on enthusing, encouraging, and empowering employees.

To further invite trust, the employees who worked with customers, as stated previously, were called Value Creators. The name helped create and sustain the notion that each individual should be encouraged to make a difference. To emphasise the point, the remainder of the organisation's departments, those not working directly with customers like HR, Marketing, Legal Services, Back Office, etc. were renamed as Enabling Functions.

The view was that these so-called head office functions existed to enable the Value Creators to create differentiated customer value.

The next big step came in introducing an employee trouble ticket system. A trouble ticket system is a familiar tool that is associated with IT functions. For any user with an IT problem, a trouble ticket is raised, identifying the worker, the problem description, and contact details. A help desk function then receives the numbered trouble ticket and responds to the ticket until the problem is solved, and the ticket is closed.

Typically, the time between raising a trouble ticket and closing the ticket is measured by a Service Level Agreement (SLA) that varies according to the severity of the problem. Problems affecting business are given shorter time to fix than problems that are more of an inconvenience.

One of the main drivers to convince the Value Creators that the company was serious about encouraging them to release their value-added ideas in customer engagements was to introduce a trouble ticket system on employee issues. The tickets were raised online by the employee and sent to the appropriate Enabling Function for resolution within an associated time limit. The online platform was called the Self Service Desk (SSD). The rules were that any employee could raise a trouble ticket on any of the Enabling Functions. The Enabling Functions had a Service Level Agreement (SLA) that gave a timeline by which the ticket needed to be responded to. The only person who could close the ticket (query resolved) was the employee, and not the Enabling Function or line manager.

Managers were measured based on the number of tickets raised by their team and the SLA response compliance. This proved to be effective for ensuring the employees' understanding that the empowerment to deliver differentiated customer value was real. In the first few months after releasing the Self Service Desk ticket system, thousands of issues and complaints poured in, from trivial issues on parking access to problems with training, company shortcomings, and missed business opportunities. Within five years, the company was receiving twenty thousand tickets a month! As I used to say, 'that is 20,000 things wrong with HCL

every month but 20,000 people who cared enough to tell us!'
The foundation of engaging, enthusing, and empowering
employees to deliver differentiated customer value was now
nearly complete.

I have met many companies that understand that they have
three major groups of stakeholders: employees, customers,
and shareholders. Too often, the decision on the top priority is
confused.

- The customer is king.
- The company only exists to deliver shareholder (or
  stakeholders for mutual companies) value.
- Our people are our most important asset.

Are all the three of equal priority? By contrast, HCL adopted a
natural hierarchy that is appropriate for a service company. If
the employees deliver differentiated customer value, the
customers will likely be more loyal and increase their
expenditure. If that happens, the shareholder value will
increase, one, two, three. Employees first, customers second,
and happy shareholders as a result.

HCL was virtually there. The final part was to answer the first
question: Did HCL deliver differentiated customer value? In
order to prove the hypothesis, it had to be measured. So, the
company introduced a Customer Value Portal. This is the only
institutionalised and industrialised customer value
measurement that I have ever come across in IT. When
meeting customers and industry analysts, I would ask them if
they knew of another such industrialised customer value
system. To date, the answer has been a unanimous 'no'.

The measurement system was introduced, whereby a piece of customer work, normally a project, could not be closed or signed off without the project team conceiving value-added ideas as a consequence of the work that they did. For example, if the work was to develop some software for a defined outcome, then the implicit expectation was that the work would be done to the agreed quality, time, and cost that were in the contract. But during the process of developing the software, the team would learn much about the way that the overall system worked, the application interfaces, dependencies, and performance. Before closing the project within HCL, the Value Creators would record suggestions for further improvement to the immediately surrounding application eco-system. Ideas on how the number of interfaces could be reduced and how elements of the eco-system could be rationalised or improved were then recorded and vetted inside HCL by the line management and system experts. The tangible benefit of implementing the idea was estimated with supporting evidence, and those material ideas that passed the HCL internal approval were submitted to the customer. The customer was asked to review the suggestions and either approve, reject, or park the idea. If the idea was approved and implemented by the customer, it was 'banked' in the Customer Value Portal as value delivered in excess of the contract.

Thus, quarterly and annually, HCL teams could demonstrate to their customers the value of the ideas and proposals that were accepted and signed off by the customers themselves in excess of the contracted requirements. These sums of differentiated customer value were then reviewed and discussed at executive steering meetings with the customers' team. The application example is only one out of many types of customer value. Each value-added idea was placed under one of the following headings:

- Cost optimisation
- Cycle time reduction
- Process improvement
- Tool development
- Technical solutions

Thus, in the customer reviews, the total value signed off by the customer could be discussed, including the spread across the value headings. This became the major proof of delivering differentiated customer value, signed off by the customer and banked. By 2016, the value realised across customers who had a Customer Value Portal was over $470 million. The circle had been squared; by encouraging, enthusing, and empowering employees to deliver differentiated customer value, HCL had become a market leader. As stated previously, the details of this journey is recorded in the book entitled *Employee First – Customer Second*, turning conventional management upside down' authored by Vineet Nayar and published by Harvard Business Press (ISBN 978-1-4221-3906-6.)

By being involved in this journey personally, I became liberated from having to have all the answers myself. If I could encourage, enthuse, and empower my team, I would trust that they would have the answers and deliver differentiated performance. And they did, year after year. The team I managed grew from single-digit million annual revenue to over $500 million and reached the milestone of $1 billion in orders in a single year. At first, the notion of empowering people seems a bit scary, but over time, it has proved to me to be the most efficient way of solving problems, addressing issues, and improving performance.

That is why, when Brian came into my office on that day, it was not long before he realised that he was going to be empowered to solve the issue that was the cause of his frustration. My role was to act as a validator and facilitator. This role is important regardless of whether a corporate transformation catalyst like that described is undertaken. We can all enthuse, encourage, and empower teams for improved success. It will also improve your Personal Share Price when you no longer need to have all the answers.

A key skill in the mix of managerial liberation from having all the answers is to listen and question.

Listening is a real skill that most of us find difficult. Listening actively and attentively is even more difficult. The proof that you have listened to something can be verified by the questions that you ask to confirm understanding. A simple, effective, and brilliant tool, in addition to questioning, is the use of paraphrasing what you have heard. Questions are appropriate to ensure that the issue that needs a decision has been well thought through. 'How do you see it working?', 'What obstacles do you think you will have to overcome?', and 'What approvals do you think you will need to begin?' are some of the questions.

Once you have understood the issue or proposition, it is then truly valuable to paraphrase what you have heard. I usually start with 'so if I have understood your issue/proposition/concern... I believe you are saying...' The veracity of the paraphrased summary will then either be confirmed or not. If not, then further explanation will be invited and the questioning and paraphrased summary can begin a second time.

I cannot overemphasise the value of listening actively and attentively. Do you listen to music or do you hear it? Do you listen to others or do you hear them? Just count the number of times that your colleagues interrupt each other before finishing a point—too often in my experience. The natural temptation is for us to hear (not listen) to the first few sentences and then assume the remainder of what the point is. This was a particular issue when talking to many Indian colleagues that I worked with – eager to please, eager to get going, and so happy to interrupt! As I have said to many a colleague, we have two ears and one mouth, and we should use them in that proportion.

So, having listened actively and attentively to understand the issues being raised and confirmation of the paraphrased summary, the journey to a solution can begin. Here, I can return to where this section started. Once Brian had articulated his point about a deeply flawed process that had been listened to actively and attentively, he himself realised that he was probably best placed to initiate actions and seek support for improving the process. In this case, the manager-subordinate trust had reached a very sophisticated level, whereby empowerment was assumed and questioning and paraphrasing were not required!

There is another benefit of enthusing, encouraging, and empowering people to solve problems. When they realise that they are likely to become involved in finding the solution to their issues, complaints diminish and default to only important issues.

Thus, creating an environment where employees feel enthused and encouraged to share their issues with you as their manager is ever more important in the age of rampant social media and the millennial generation. I was once told that the millennial or Y generation should in fact be called the 'why' generation as they question everything. Listening actively and attentively will convince them that you are serious about hearing them out. Questioning and paraphrasing to confirm understanding are further proof that you care. From this understanding, you can ask what ideas the employee has on resolving the issue and who should be involved. This will invariably require that the employees themselves are part of providing the solution, or indeed, leading the charge.

As the technique of creating an empowered environment, listening, questioning, and paraphrasing developed, my role became one of establishing a platform from which each individual would be enthused, encouraged, and empowered to initiate the solution to their own problems to a considerable extent. If this required other participants, then the empowerment extended to connecting the right people to share the concern and agree to develop the solution.

This is just a small example of what happens when people feel empowered. A whole reservoir of ideas is released, issues are aired, and the people are empowered to solve problems alone or with others.

There is an analogy, which I developed, that works well to summarise this notion. It is that champagne bubbles come from the bottom of the glass, and not the top. As to why the champagne bubbles get released, the answer is they are initiated from tiny particles of dirt that cannot be seen with the naked eye. These microscopic dirt particles are what the bubbles are created from. So, similarly, irritations and issues in a business act like the dirt particles to stimulate bubbles of ideas. I always found this analogy to be powerful in imagining the endless potential in the people I worked with.

This section highlights the opportunity to become more liberated in management and lessen the need for managers to feel that they need to have the answers to all questions. However, this does not replace the requirement for managers to be accountable to the franchise they have. The techniques that I have described are in addition to good management practices that have been much written about, and for which there are numerous training courses. Furthermore, the techniques that I have described do not require that employees are empowered within a regime like *Employee First*. As a manager of your own business unit or team, such techniques can be introduced, and they will work as they depend more on the managers' attitude to their own teams than a centralised transformation programme. That attitude is wrapped in presence, behaviour, and performance and valued within a Personal Share Price (PSP).

Liberation summary:

- Aim to become a liberated manager by enthusing, encouraging, and empowering the people in your team to realise their full potential.
- Believe that everyone is better than they think they are. That includes you.
- Invite trust in your team and others by being transparent in all your dealings.
- The team's job is to deliver differentiated customer value, facilitated by you. Develop a means of measuring differentiated customer value in your team, and share it with customers. Note that the customers can be external *and* internal to your company.
- You do not have to have all the answers. You are liberated when others volunteer to solve the issues that they face.
- Listen actively and attentively. Question and paraphrase to confirm that you have listened and understood. This shows that you care.
- Good ideas are like champagne bubbles. They come from the bottom, and not the top, and are stimulated by 'dirt' (imperfections). Encourage your team to release their bubbles of ideas.
- When you work with people from a younger generation, take the trouble to understand their world and how they interact with others.
- Monitor the impact of your actions on your PSP to ensure sustained momentum.

- Remember you do not have to have all the answers and your team will be grateful for the empowerment you facilitate

Liberation from your cultural heritage

We live in a multi-cultural society where global travel is affordable for many people. Social media is the catalyst for international connections that were unavailable to previous generations. It is our duty to be open to learning about different cultures both in business and in life. Ignorance too often results in laughable outcomes, parodied by comedians or worse yet triggering international incidents. Making the effort to understand different cultures and, perhaps more importantly, to understand one's own culture in the context of other cultures represent the 'table stakes' today. Those more enlightened managers will have a superior presence and behave appropriately in the vast majority of cultural experiences. Be assured that developing cultural awareness will have a positive impact on your PSP inside and outside work. Cultural awareness is exhibited in both a corporate context as well as in a geopolitical context. There are numerous books and training courses on cultural awareness that I am unqualified to cover. Instead, I offer my personal experiences and the impact that they had on my behaviour, presence, and performance.

In my career, I have worked for four global organisations – three quoted companies and one consulting partnership – and a Dotcom startup. These organisations were based in USA, Europe, and India and represented in up to 90 countries. While working in these organisations, one becomes cognizant of the cultural differences that make each company or organisation unique. The way that large global companies develop inevitably creates a corporate personality in addition to the culture that is associated with the parent company's head office location.

It is important when joining a company that the individual makes efforts to understand the corporate personality and what makes the organisation work. Be clear to distinguish the individual corporate culture from the national culture of the organisation. They are distinct layers. The national culture underpins the corporate culture, but the corporate culture changes with new senior executives and with strategic or transformative initiatives. In fact, some company cultures are so strong that they can thwart the attempts for a major transformation. When I worked at Prudential Corporation, we considered the need to get through 'the middle management treacle', as we called it, to ensure that a strategic change succeeded.

One way of illuminating a specific corporate culture is to ask to examine an organisational diagram of a company. The chairman and CEO are at the top with various business unit heads and support function heads reporting in: Sales, Marketing, Manufacturing, Delivery, HR, Finance, Legal, Regulatory, and Compliance, and so on.

From this chart, you can ask, 'but how does the company work?' In other words, does it work in a federated model with each business unit being essentially autonomous, or is the company controlled entirely from the centre? Is the company led by marketing, sales, finance, or HR? Find out who the most powerful people in the organisation are. This will begin to inform you about the psyche of the company. In short, the formal organisation diagram is rarely a guide to how the company works. Soon revealed are the large individual personalities in the company who hold a disproportionate sway among the leadership. All or most of the expected caricatures in business will be there.

In addition, there is a marked cultural element that is more obvious, which is based on the country and city of the head office. Having worked for US, UK, Scandinavian, and Indian companies, I can assure you that it is vital to understand the cultural differences in order to prosper. The strange but obvious point is that for people who have grown up in a given country, there is a natural but unwise conclusion that one's own culture is 'right' and all others are at best a deviation from the norm.

I recall a story that a friend of mine once told me. Richard Edwards OBE was an executive member of an international hotel and catering trade association. As part of his duties, he organised an annual conference in a prestigious location. This included arranging transport from hotels to conference venues. He said that when delegates were asked to be on the coach from the hotel by 8:30 am, the following would happen. The British, Germans, and Scandinavians would arrive no later than 8:15 am. Then, the Japanese, Australians, Americans, and New Zealanders would arrive at 8:30 am precisely. The French, southern Europeans, and Chinese would appear about fifteen minutes later, and finally, the South Americans would wander down at around 9:15 am. It serves as an amusing metaphor for cultural difference.

One of the joys that I have had in my working life is to try to understand different cultures in contrast to my own native culture, being British born and bred. I did, however, have some early experience of cultural difference as I spent the first ten years of my life with my parents in Africa. I recall one episode when my mother went to a hairdresser. She had bought a wig in England and had taken it to a local hairdresser in Nigeria to be beautified for a forthcoming do. The following day, she returned as arranged. When she arrived, there was a large group of excited women waiting outside the hairdresser's shop. The story had got around that a European woman had actually left her hair at the hairdressers and walked away! The locals could not believe how this could be done and came to witness the wonder! At the time, these women had never seen or heard of a wig.

There was another example when my parents hosted a drinks party. Canapés were available, including small sausages on a stick. When my mother noticed that the sausages had not arrived, she went to the kitchen and found the cook, with a needle and thread, sewing the sausages that had split their skin! You see, my mother had earlier made clear to the cook the need to be careful in the cooking of the sausages as she did not want to serve sausages with split skins to her guests. The cook had found the solution from a different cultural context.

By way of illustration of cultural difference nowadays, I refer to the use of the word, 'yes'. In USA, 'yes' is most often assumed as 'it will be done'. In UK, it can mean 'I understand'. In India, there is a to and fro sideways head movement for 'yes' and a more vigorous movement for 'very yes'. In other countries, 'yes' can mean 'I hear you' or 'that sounds reasonable'.

Even this one simple word can be the cause of immense frustration. I recall an American friend of mine, Barry, coming to the UK. He was a mature businessman who had developed a product that would guarantee that a company could not have its internal phone system hacked. This was in the late 1990s, when criminals could hack into a company's internal phone system and run up huge telecommunication bills, connecting people across the globe for a fee. The product worked, was proven in the USA, and was backed by insurance in the unlikely event that the hackers prevailed. Over several months and customer presentation after presentation, my friend became very excited at the positive response. I would often hear him say that 'they had said *yes* to my proposal.' But month after month, the orders did not materialise. In the end, I explained that saying 'yes' and meaning they will place an order were two very different things in the UK. After eighteen months, he left in deep frustration at trying to do business in the UK and withdrew back to the USA. He just could not adjust to a different way of doing business. The only benchmark that he had was how business was conducted in the USA. Three months later, Barry phoned me to say that one of his hot UK prospects had called him, saying that they had been hacked for £250,000 in one month and needed his device! My friend took great delight in telling them: 'I am out of the business in the UK; thank you for your call and best of luck.' So, cultural difference got the better of my friend, but perhaps he had the last laugh.

I have made genuine attempts to assimilate cultural difference when doing business, but even this has been met with one case of complete failure. This is the case of doing business in France. There is something about that country's culture that I have never found the key to. I have tried with different companies, different times, different propositions, different people, but I always had the same result – failure – and I am sure it was due to my inability to crack the code of doing business in France.

When I employed a French national to begin our business in HCL, I related my failure to do business in France and genuinely wished him well. In fact, I said I would eat my hat if he could do some business in his first six months. Five months later, he called me to gloat over the fact that he had secured his first contract and reminded me of my promise to eat my hat. I was duly chastened and congratulated him in all humility. A few weeks later, I called to speak to him, and his office said he was in London. Somewhat confused, I called him on his mobile. He answered, and I asked what he was doing in London. 'Ah', he said, the contract that he had won was for a French company's business in UK. Can you regurgitate a hat!

Once one becomes accustomed to cultural differences, a vast world opens up – one's own prejudices are exposed, and a new foundation for interacting with 'foreigners' is established – accepting that we ourselves are 'foreigners' to everyone else.

Another entertaining example to illustrate cultural difference is again from the USA. A colleague and I were returning home from a conference in Orlando, Florida. We were near the departure gate at the airport when we noticed that there was a small bar across the way. The two of us had passed the 21st anniversary of our 21st birthday and looked it. I approached the bar and asked the lady for two beers. With a straight face, she asked to see our ID. We both laughed and thanked her for making our day. The beers did not come. I asked again, and she repeated the request for the IDs. We were at an international airport, so we produced our passports, which she studied and returned, and then poured the beers. Out of curiosity, I asked her why she needed to see our ID as we were obviously of mature years. She replied 'that way I do not have to decide who is over 21 and who isn't.' In most countries, a more commonsensical visual qualification would more likely have sufficed, but the logic of the lady's response was infallible.

It was further evidence of a notion that I had developed, and which has stood me in good stead ever since I recognised it. I offer this to help ameliorate the trap of assumptions across different cultures. The notion is that when you see, hear, or read something from a culture that is different from your own, which to you is bizarre, weird, laughable, or plain daft, ask yourself, 'What has to be true for that to be reasonable?'

In the case of the airport beers, it was simple. The lady did not want to be responsible for assuming someone's age, however strange it might seem. Who knows, she might have got it wrong once, through a commonsensical judgement, and may have been reprimanded or worse. So I repeat, ask yourself – what has to be true, for a particular circumstance that you find bizarre or strange, to be reasonable. Answering this question, however crudely, has broadened my insight into cultural difference. The 'what has to be true' test can be used to better understand behaviours and experiences across all different cultures.

The insight that I gained on 'what has to be true' was hugely influential in my introduction to HCL on April Fools' Day in 2004. April Fool's Day is an annual celebration for practical jokes, so I should have been on alert. I was the fourth European to join HCL and the longest serving non-Indian till date. In the early days, there were behaviours and things said, which, quite frankly, astonished me. 'Why do they do that?', 'How do they get business with that approach?', and 'How do they come to that conclusion?' were some of the questions that occurred to me. To illustrate the point, it is well known with some humour that Indian people are pre-disposed to answer 'yes' (there it is again) to any and all closed questions. Why do they always say yes?

Applying the 'what has to be true' test, a visit to India will expose the massive polarisation of almost all elements of life – extreme wealth and extreme poverty side by side. Traffic chaos that is so extreme that, it is, in fact, efficient! Hundreds of millions below the World Bank's definition of poverty in the world's largest democracy that has 900 million people voting electronically. This when Europe struggles with postal vote abuse, and the USA has had problems with chads. In India, there are wine shops that do not sell wine, ISO 9001 certified gentlemen's hairdressers (I kid you not), and cows in the middle of the road that represent travel normalcy. In this amazing country, it is not difficult to see that all things are possible. So, 'yes, I can' is a reasonable response in almost all situations. What was not asked is, what was assumed in order to achieve the goal? In my own culture, we put undeclared conditions on our answers like the cost, time, likelihood of success, and other conditions before we answer. However, in other cultures, no such preconditions may apply. Maybe they assume no constraints at all, in which case all things are possible. In this context, India is a country where all things are possible; so, 'yes' is a reasonable answer to almost any closed question.

The lesson learnt from understanding this Indian cultural phenomenon is never to ask a closed question. Ask what, when, how, where, and the answers will have less cultural frustration for westerners. I say 'have less', because a willingness to please is also deeply embedded in Indian culture. Ask a driver how long it will take to arrive at a destination – the answer will generally be forty-five minutes. In truth, he has no clue, and in the chaotic traffic, it is a stupid question for westerners to ask. But, in order to please, the driver knows that thirty minutes will not be believed and one hour sounds too long. There, you are satisfied – in complete ignorance!

I could say – don't get me started on my own native culture. The British may well be among the worst cases of being misunderstood across cultures. Two linguistic elements, irony and sarcasm, are used to such an extent that they only serve to confuse most people not brought up in Britain. Be careful when someone says 'that is a lovely shirt you are wearing'. If the emphasis is on 'lovely', it probably means that they do not like it or it is gross. As the Americans would say – go figure. I do not intend to delve deeper into the British cultural idiosyncrasies. Suffice it to say that they are pervasive, and, as in the example quoted, counter intuitive. Worse still, it leaves the receiver unsure of whether a compliment or a put-down has been offered.

Cultural difference, make no mistake, is essential to take into account when managing or interacting with employees, colleagues, and customers. My simple proposition in order to help is to ask yourself – what has to be true for that response, point of view, or proposition to be reasonable. This will, in my experience, save one from countless waking hours and frustration and positively impact one's PSP.

We all grow up with an ingrained cultural orientation that, in adulthood, becomes the norm against which we judge others because our upbringing in most cases is centred around one family, one country, one religion, one political system, and one ethos. This combined is why we each derive comfort from being at 'home'. Home has many connotations, but it is where we feel most comfortable with ourselves, surrounded by people who understand us best, in an environment that we have grown up in.

When we experience different cultures, we often struggle to assimilate different ideas, benchmarks, behaviours, and ways of life. Cecil Rhodes, businessman and politician of the late ninetieth century, is reported to have said, 'to be born English is to win first prize in the lottery of life.' If that were true, all other countries are by definition relative losers. Nonetheless, it is clear where he stood – for the subjugation of tribal cultures in Africa.

More recently, there were two well-reported incidents highlighting cultural differences involving the famous footballer Lionel Messi. The first was when a five-year-old Afghan boy was shown wearing a shirt fashioned out of a blue-striped plastic bag with Messi's name on it. The image went viral on the internet, and shortly afterwards, the boy received a real shirt signed by Messi. The boy said, 'I love Messi and my shirt says Messi loves me.' Thus, through a happy event, Messi's Personal Share Price went even higher than normal. However, only a few weeks later, all things changed and Messi's PSP took a hit. This time, Messi donated a pair of his football boots for a charity auction in Egypt. This quickly invoked a great offence to the Egyptian people. 'We (Egyptians) have never been so humiliated during our seven thousand years of civilization', said Said Hasasin, a parliament member and TV presenter. The controversy centres on the significance of shoes in Arab culture. Considered one of the lowliest of items, because it literally touches the ground, many Egyptians find it a dirty and inappropriate object. To call someone a 'gazma', the Arabic word for shoe, is a great insult. And if someone catches sight of your soles, if you have your feet up, you are sure to pay the price. On one occasion in 2008 during an Iraqi press conference, a journalist threw one of his shoes at the USA President Bush as an insult. Thus, in these last few examples, the positive and negative power of cultural difference becomes very apparent.

I find it is useful to test myself in how culturally aware I am, and it is a useful self-learning discipline. Among the questions are the following:

- When was the last time you asked someone what their Christian name was? Should that be the given name?

- When was the last time you spoke to someone whose given name was their second name? Did you know it?
- Are you aware of the major world religions? Do you know something of the dos and don'ts in those religions?
- How many languages can you speak? If none other than your native tongue, in how many languages can you say 'yes', 'no', and 'thank you'? One should make an effort.
- What do you know about the history and political structure of the countries that you work in or visit?
- Are you aware of the customs and behaviours that can offend in the countries that you have visited or worked with?

These are just a few obvious points of reference, but be assured that the world is increasingly multi-cultural. A few years ago, when I met a young person, I used to ask how many Facebook friends they had. Frequently, the answer was in the hundreds. At the time, if I sent 150 Christmas cards to my friends and family, I felt well connected! Of more interest now is to ask a young adult how many nationalities are represented in their Facebook or other social media contact list. In my experience, the answer is frequently in the tens. The millennial generation is clearly at a level of international dialogue and cultural awareness that was largely unavailable to their parents. As I travel the world, I have noticed that most people under 25 years of age seem to dress similarly and listen to the same music, and people over 55 years of age dress in a more traditional way and listen to music more associated with their historical culture. In my own country, this became very visible when the Brexit vote occurred in June 2016. The majority of under 25s voted to remain as part of the European Union, and the majority of over 55s voted for leaving.

Twenty years ago, very few people in the UK knew what the Hindu festival of Diwali was. Now, it is an annual international news item on the BBC, and most people in Britain know that it is the Hindu festival of light. So, spending time assimilating a rudimentary understanding of different cultures has, for me, been a most rewarding addition to the work and enjoyment of daily life. But I still use the 'what has to be true' test to protect me from tripping up too often.

As a very recent example, I flew to Delhi and a car collected me to take me to a hotel. I noticed a small, credit card–sized printed label attached to the shoulder strap of the passenger seat belt. On it, the following was written:

The amenities in your car:

1. Two bottles of mineral water
2. Daily newspaper
3. Chauffeur with mobile phone
4. First Aid kit
5. Umbrella
6. Coat hanger
7. Mobile phone charger
8. Hammer

No. 8 was worth a chuckle, but the 'what has to be true' test indicated that there were means of combating external aggression or breaking a window to escape in an emergency. I came to the view that it was for the passenger's peace of mind, but someone had thought about it, put it on the list, and thought it to be reasonable, if not a good idea.

But before becoming too complacent, I am reminded of my faux pas in France. I had been invited to Paris to accept an award on behalf of Vineet Nayar from The Foundation Manpower that recognises managers who have contributed to innovative management practices. There was an audience of around 300 people from various companies and business schools from across France. I was given a translator to work with, who translated the short speech that I gave and the responses to the Q&A session. One interesting aspect of the French and English languages is that words ending in -tion are generally the same. Thus, the word 'communication' is the same in both the languages, notwithstanding differences in pronunciation. Similarly, 'observation' and other -tion words are the same. My mistake was that in describing the innovative management practices used at HCL, I used the word 'collaboration' once or twice in the context of employees working together for the benefit of customers. Collaboration is the same word in French, and so, was recognisable without translation. After accepting the award and enjoying the applause on behalf of Vineet, I retired to my seat for the chairman of the event to close the session. Afterwards, I was invited to stay for a drink and answer any further questions from the attendees. This went well until a kind gentleman came up to me and told me that in future, if I address a French audience, I should use the word 'cooperation' instead of 'collaboration'. He said 'unfortunately the word collaboration has a bad meaning in France from the time of the last war when some notables in France "collaborated" with the Nazis'. I subsequently learnt that after the Second World War, over 6,700 collaborators were sentenced to death in France and a further 49,000 were sentenced to 'national degradation' – a loss of face and civil rights. This reminded me of how sensitive people can be to the most innocent of cultural references.

One other point about India is worth mentioning in the context of cultural difference and innovation. This philosophy has had books written about it, and the august Harvard Business Review covered the concept under the heading of Frugal Innovation. The term is *Jugaad,* which will cause a smile to appear on the face of any Indian you mention it to. This is a sign that you have indeed reached a deeper level of Indian cultural awareness.

If you have ever visited India, you will see many engineering phenomena that, by western standards, should never work. Some road vehicles have been cobbled together from different chassis, engines, exhaust systems, seating, roofing, and storage. These are the Frankensteins of the road. You will see this concept repeated with water pumps, cooling fans, and devices of all shades in domestic and small business environments. It is an ingrained and evident part of Indian culture.

On January 25, 2010, Harvard Business Review effectively legitimised this make-do-and-mend practice by publishing a paper entitled: *Jugaad: A New Growth Formula for Corporate America*. The opening paragraph read as follows:

'Frugal innovation is a hot topic today as post-downturn corporate America looks for ways to do more for less, while serving broader markets. This will require practising the gutsy art of Jugaad. The Hindi term roughly translates as "overcoming harsh constraints by improvising an effective solution using limited resources". We call it the art of creative improvisation—within a framework of deep knowledge and experience.'

To emphasise the relevance of Jugaad, a book was published in 2012 entitled *Jugaad Innovation*, by Carlos Ghosn, CEO of Renault-Nissan. The sub-heading is *Think Frugal, Be Flexible, Generate Breakthrough Growth*.

The concept of Jugaad has thus transcended cultures and goes some way to explain the 'yes' response to almost any closed question posed to an Indian.

For those interested in learning more about cultural difference in a business context, there are two recommended books. The first is entitled *Fish Can't See Water,* written by Kai Hammerich and Richard D. Lewis. The book explores the impact of national culture on corporate strategy and its execution, and through this, the impact on business. It does not argue that different cultures lead to different business results, but that all cultures impact organisations in both positive and negative ways, depending on the business cycle, the particular business, and the particular strategies being pursued. Depending on all of these factors, cultural dynamics can either enable or derail performance. But recognising those cultural factors is difficult for business leaders; like everyone else, they too can be blind to the culture of which they are a part. The second book for a deeper understanding of cultural difference is *Riding the Waves of Culture: Understanding Diversity in Global Business*, written by Frons Trompenaars and Charles Hampden. They spent ten years researching people in various global cultures. They surveyed 46,000 managers in 40 countries and concluded that people from different cultures express preferences based on seven dimensions. The model can be used to prevent misunderstandings and enjoy a better working relationship with people from different cultures.

As a more informal illustration of cultural difference, I always think of the example of international plugs and sockets. It seems that almost every country has a different system for connecting electrical goods: round pin, square pin, two pin, three pin, flat pin, angled pin and so on, not forgetting the different voltages. Thus, when I travel, I ask myself if I am carrying the metaphoric universal travel plug adaptor of cultural awareness or if I will remain frustrated at how often I cannot connect. Thus, it is very appropriate to conclude with – be prepared to adapt as you travel.

Liberation summary:

- Liberate yourself from your own cultural shell of experience. Be open to difference.
- Distinguish between company and country cultures, and understand that the way that a company works is not how it is structured.
- Beware of simple words like 'yes'; it may not mean what you think it means.
- Accept that you are a foreigner to everyone outside your own country, religion, creed,

education, and upbringing. As Robert Louis Stevenson wrote: there is no foreign land, it is the traveller only that is foreign.

- When behaviours from otherwise sensible people seem bizarre or daft, apply the 'what has to be true' test to gain cultural understanding and reduce frustration.
- If in doubt, think of Lionel Messi and international plugs and sockets.
- Be aware that cultural concepts like Jugaad may have a place in your organisation.
- Become adaptable and willing to learn about other cultures even within your own country.
- Monitor your cultural experiences and ability to assimilate cultural difference on your PSP.

Liberation and animal instincts

Change is the new black, as I recently read from a website called *Untethered Thinking*. Our ability to cope with change is an increasingly important facet of management. Furthermore, our ability to recognise changing patterns and adapt our behaviour and performance is even more crucial in today's dynamic business environment. The paradox is that we learn from our experiences and that, in turn, moulds our behaviour. Unlearning experiences and being open to new ideas, probably not yours, are the more important skills for the future. This is frequently the frustration between generations in families. Although order and chaos are not natural bedfellows, they are both vital to performance based on innovation.

Another challenge for managers is that as the world changes ever faster, the temptation to take on more work and responsibility grows. Learning to manage this tendency is important for one's longer-term well-being.

To illustrate these issues and their impact on PSP, I found that a comparison with some animal behaviours helped me understand how I could better deal with work demands, keep up with change, and encourage innovation. The examples of behaviour from elephants, monkeys, dinosaurs and birds are offered as an engaging way of looking at familiar issues from a different perspective.

Learning from elephants

Why do elephants not break their tethering rope? The answer is in fact straightforward. Young elephants, in countries where they grow to be the industrial machines of rural industry, are tethered. From the earliest of years, they are tethered to ensure that they do not roam. These young elephants make some attempts to escape the tether, but they eventually give up as the tether for a young elephant is too strong. When the elephant grows to full adulthood, the conditioning is well set. They are so used to being tethered that they do not attempt to escape. However, a fully grown elephant could easily lose its tether. If only they knew how powerful they are, they would know what freedom is. But they don't.

Similarly, we humans become accustomed to our limitations whether set in our youth or later. 'I can't' is far too often said by young people as is 'I am not clever', 'I can't do that', 'I am no good at football', and so on. By the time adulthood arrives, the competency tethering is complete. This is one reason why true innovation, as opposed to development, is a challenge for the vast majority of us after, say, thirty years of age. I learnt in my fourties that if I thought of an innovative idea, it probably wasn't one. True innovation is distinct from evolution, major developments, or bright ideas. To illustrate this point, I believe that no conventionally trained chief financial officer (CFO) of fourty years of age or more would have approved the business case for Facebook, Twitter, or Google, or many other true innovations of the internet age. The business case would just not stack up against the criteria that are ingrained in a mature CFO. Of course, there are exceptions to the rule, but they should be considered as rare.

I once attended a World Economic Forum meeting in Vienna. One of the themes of the conference was innovation. I had been asked to speak on a panel because my company had completed its fifth year of the innovative management culture called Employee First Customer Second (EFCS), referred to earlier. The book of the same name had become a best seller. The philosophy and impact on improved business performance were, thanks to the book, of international interest to business leaders from all industries.

Included in the conference agenda was a plenary session on innovation in business. Three well-known organisations spoke about how they encourage innovation in their workforce. The common theme seemed to be creating a forum for innovative ideas supported by a business plan that would be submitted to an internal panel in each company. The panel would select a small number of ideas for the proposers to attend a Q & A session before finally selecting one or two of the ideas to invest in.

In the end, I could not help myself, as none of the speakers were under thirty years of age, and neither was I.

When questions were put to the floor, my hand went up. I simply asked, 'what was the average age of the panellists choosing the most worthwhile innovations?' There was bewilderment at the question, so I elaborated by asking how many of the panellists, deciding on the innovation proposals, were thirty years or younger. Not one of the organisations had a single panellist under thirty. I then admitted that my own age and experience would, I contend, rule me out of recognising truly game-changing innovation (due to the tethered elephant conditioning). I then rather cheekily suggested that the presenters should encourage their companies to discard the chosen ideas and take out those that were first put in the bin and re-examine them, as that is where the gold most likely lay. I do not think my point was given any credence. But I remain committed to the idea that tethered thinking stifles innovation, and our role is to foster innovation and allow the younger employees to decide what ideas might bear the most fruit and support them.

As an example, in HCL, the company announced an innovation ideas forum called MADJAM (Make A Difference JAMboree). MADJAM was an annual event, during which all non-managerial employees were invited to develop ideas and propositions to 'make a difference'. There was no restriction on the type of idea, ranging from philanthropic to business improvement propositions. Each idea would be registered on the intranet through a formal template. The propositions were then socialised by the idea initiators using broadcast emails and various in-company promotion activities, like canteen display stands. The ideas were promoted for two months. Then, all the employees were invited to vote for the idea that they thought was the best. Typically, over 10,000 HCLites participated in the voting. The idea that received the most votes from the employees, not managers, was obliged to be invested in by the company. Among the ideas that succeeded was the sponsored planting of trees at orphanages across India, and at least two other ideas that developed into $100 million business units over three years. Thus, as opposed to a learned panel, employees chose the investment ideas. The average age of HCL employees at the time was about 27 years of age. These were the least tethered thinkers by my definition.

Monkey business

In 1998, I attended the General Management course at Ashridge Management College in England. There was an expected array of topics to discuss and learn: finance, marketing, sales, administration, HR, and so on. However, there was one lecture that became a watershed in my management thinking and behaviour from that day. We were a group of some thirty senior managers from all industries and had been selected as future boardroom material. It was a fun group, and for various tasks, we were assigned into groups. Our group was called the 'Winners' (no sense in aiming low, right?). At the end of the course, around the time of Christmas, each group provided some entertainment for the others. In our case, we played instruments and sang festively appropriate Christmas carols. The point was that the learning was designed with fun in mind.

One memorable session began quite normally with the lecturer coming into the lowly lit theatre where the class was sitting and introduced himself. As he approached the lectern, the group gradually noticed something odd. Some immediately began to giggle because on his back there was a metre-high stuffed toy monkey. Its arms were secured around the lecturer's neck at the front. As we began to point and laugh, he would turn around and see nothing. This went on for a few minutes until he eventually stood still, and we calmed down. He then asked one of our colleagues, sitting at the front, if he wouldn't mind staying behind after the lecture to collect materials and tidy up, as he had an urgent meeting to attend immediately after the session. Our colleague agreed. The lecturer then took the monkey from his back and put it on the back of the colleague who had agreed to stay back.

The monkey was, in fact, a visible metaphor for carrying a burden.

The lecture then began in earnest. The point was that many of us in life carry too many monkeys on our backs. Indeed, some people you meet are so burdened by work or life that they seem to carry tens of monkeys on their backs. Other people appear to sail through life or work without a care and treat the one or two monkeys they have as pets rather than pests.

This really hit me between the eyes. I immediately began to imagine myself, my work colleagues, and family with monkeys on their backs. The trick became to tame or share the monkeys or to give them to someone else. It was a graphic lesson in understanding the art of delegation, and also the art of empowering people to accept more responsibility and to grow in their environments. You see, not all monkeys are bad, and the more monkeys that can be nurtured, fostered, and found a home for, the more we can grow as people. So, we can take some monkeys off our backs and release them in a forest under our care to be enjoyed and used as we needed. Distinguishing bad monkeys that burden and provide no joy from the ones that enrich and are fun to play with becomes a key skill as we develop.

As an illustration, a charming man, called Sandip, once worked in my team as a salesman. He was an excellent salesman with great customer connections, an engaging personality, and a good sense of humour. Everyone liked Sandip. But he just wanted to play with the fun-loving sales monkey. He hated administration of any sort. He once let his expenses lapse for nine months! Despite me telling him he was funding the company, he did not put in the effort to reclaim his money, which was spent on behalf of the company. To him, paperwork, in all its forms, was a bad monkey that was best never dealt with. He just did not want to tame it, nurture it, and keep it in his jungle of tamed capabilities. It cost him several thousand pounds a year to indulge his dislike of the administration monkey that grew ever larger on his back.

The lesson for me is that monkeys will come your way, they will land on your back, sometimes several at a time. The skill is to quickly get rid of the ones that do not enhance your potential or well-being and to tame, nurture, and foster those monkeys that add to your capability and well-being.

Today, as I get to know work colleagues, I can imagine the ones with many irritating monkeys on their back, but like the lecturer, they cannot see them. There are also colleagues with a cheerful monkey or two on their backs and some others on a lead, and those colleagues with no monkeys on their back but a forest full of happy monkeys that they can take for a piggyback anytime.

The monkey concept also went some way in explaining why some people can handle a role like being the president of their country in the same 24 hours a day that the rest of us have. They can tame a large number of monkeys themselves and employ animal handlers for other needs.

Have you looked in the mirror recently? What did you see on your back?

Beware of the dinosaurs

Another animal instinct to avoid is becoming a dinosaur. Although extinct for some 65 million years, many derivatives are alive and well in corporate life. Many of these corporate dinosaurs are difficult to identify as they adopt a human body, but their thinking and behaviours become exposed sooner or later. The time in which these creatures mostly manifest themselves is during major change programmes. When an organisation becomes convinced that it is time for a major change or transformation, the end result can be defined, but the journey towards it is often anything but clear. This is when various dinosaur characters appear that I have given names like Wellpoisonorus (Well Poisoners). Wellpoisonoruses are those individuals who are cynical, derogatory in comments, and are generally pessimistic about change. The danger with them is that they can be influential and encourage negative behaviour in others. Then there are other characters called Zombiorus (Zombies) or the walking dead, who are generally demotivated, uninterested, and are there for the payday alone. The danger with these characters is that they can suck the life out of a team. Wellpoisonoruses like to recruit Zombioruses to form a dinosaur alliance against change. I will not dwell on this as much has been written about these and other caricatures in organisations that become more distinguishable during an organisational transformation. I have never witnessed an alliance against organisational change ever succeed, but it can serve to delay and frustrate the progress.

I have been party to organisational transformations from two sides. One was through working for a global consulting company advising and guiding corporate client transformations, and the other was as an employed participant in a number of corporate transformations.

The surprising aspect of the dinosaur alliance is that too often they think that they remain unidentified through stealth. But the size of the dinosaurs makes them hard to miss!

I would like to again refer to the corporate transformation that began at HCL in 2005, this time in the context of dinosaurs with different names as they appear in the book entitled *Employee First - Customer Second*.

When the idea of transformation was first proposed by the CEO Vineet Nayar at a meeting in Delhi, three character types emerged almost immediately. There were the enthusiasts who understood the need for change and wanted to be part of the revolution; these were called the 'Transformers'. The second group were the wait-and-see brigade that were called the 'Fence Sitters'. Last were the 'Lost Souls' who would never be convinced that any change would be effective. However, this group was also vociferous and acted as energy-sapping black holes.

Recognising the three groups was important, and we knew that the transformation would succeed even if we had a marginal minority of Transformers, as the Fence Sitters were initially inactive and persuadable.

The important lesson for me is that committing wholeheartedly to a corporate transformation is the only route to fulfilment. The alternatives provide a negative or neutral environment that can never be fulfilling. Thus, behaving like a dinosaur ends only in extinction. My advice is that if you do not believe in an announced transformation and you have had your say, it is better for you and the organisation that you leave. So the next time you are asked to embrace change, embrace it; there really is nothing to lose. The worst that can happen is that you learn more about yourself.

In the HCL example, the transformation succeeded spectacularly, as there were enough Transformers; the Fence Sitters grew fewer, and enough of the Lost Souls were eventually converted. In that environment, with the dinosaurs in the minority, they could be tolerated or allowed to drift away into obscurity.

In a second example, I was a senior manager in a global merger of IT companies to create Unisys Ltd. There were two magical memories of the success of this merger. The first was a picture taken of the new board of directors a week after the merger. This was widely published within the newly formed company. In the picture were the new executive board members wearing a baseball cap with the name of the new company on it. In front of each board member were two other caps, each with the name of one of the pre-merger companies. The message was that if any of the board members mentioned either of the pre-merger company names, they would have to replace their Unisys cap with the one of the company that they mentioned. This was very effective in encouraging everyone across the globe to not dwell on the past, and it was a graphic message to the dinosaurs. There was never another picture of the board at any other time, so no one knew how many were wearing the new company cap at the end of each board meeting! In fact, it did not matter, as the message was loud and clear. The second magical memory was the pace at which the post-merger implementation happened. Within 90 days of the confirmed merger, every person of the approximately 90,000 employees knew what their role was, who their reporting manager was, and who would be at risk of redundancy with preferred terms. This was across 80 countries. When reflecting on the fact that both the pre-merger companies were competitors in most of the 80 countries with a large number of duplicate roles, 90 days was astonishingly quick. The speed of implementation did not allow for a dinosaur alliance to emerge. There were bound to be redundancies, and this is the foodstuff that dinosaurs need to thrive. Pace does not permit time for a harvest, let alone feasting and gluttony. The pace of the merger was formally recognised in the annual report of the first year. In the chairman's notes was the following remark: 'no doubt in the haste with which we moved, we made mistakes, but acting in haste was not one of them'. From my experience of this merger, I concluded henceforth that in the vast majority of cases (certainly major transformations), I would recommend pace over precision every time. Dinosaurs are, by nature, slow thinkers and movers. If you think about it, their extinction was also a question of pace 65 million years ago. Although scientists still debate about the cause, all of them agree that it was quick. Over a relatively short time, dinosaurs disappeared completely (except for some birds). Although the number of dinosaur species was already declining, a sudden catastrophic event sealed their fate, causing unfavourable changes to the environment more quickly than dinosaurs could adapt to. Except for the birds...

For the birds?

To say that something is 'for the birds' is to call it horse manure. Dating from the days of horse-drawn traffic in cities like New York and London, horse manure was a hugely unpleasant smelling problem. In the late 19th century, there were over 50,000 horses in London and 100,000 in New York. In 1894, the Times newspaper predicted, 'In 50 years, every street in London will be buried under nine feet of manure.' During this period, birds would flock to eat the undigested oats and cereals in the horse manure, and the expression 'for the birds' was born.

However, despite this unfortunate reference, there is much to learn from the behaviour of birds. Not only were they not all killed off with the dinosaurs, but they have evolved sophisticated management techniques. There are few better examples of teamwork than birds in flight. Instinctive teamwork can be observed when ducks migrate and fly in formation. Ducks represent an excellent example of individuals coming together for the good of the group. Migration distances can be as far as 14,000 km. This is a massive undertaking that requires strength and determination. We learnt from the movie *The Mighty Ducks* that 'Ducks fly together!' Later in the movie, other quotes include the following: 'And just when you think they are about to break apart – Ducks fly together' and 'When the wind blows hard and the sky is black – Ducks fly together.' By flying in a V-formation, scientists estimate that the whole flock can fly about 70% farther than they would individually, without exerting extra energy. This is because flying together helps reduce wind resistance while also providing additional lift. Similarly, teams in the workplace can achieve outstanding results without significant extra energy – 'flying together'.

Geese adopt another strategy in which, when the leader of the V-formation gets fatigued, it drops to the back to allow another member of the flock to take over the lead. The lead changes numerous times during a migration. Another phenomenon that we can learn from birds is what is called 'abmigration.' This involves birds from one migrating region joining birds from a different breeding region in a common winter location and then migrating back together as one population. I can relate to this example when considering the need to provide services to a global account present in many countries, but that require common service standards from a supplier. The customer head office location is typically where the global account management is located, but that team will need to 'fly together' with account managers in other countries to ensure maximum coverage and consistent service across the globe. They will need to fly together even when some of the remote account managers are not dedicated to the global account.

The above examples of birds' instinctive teamwork should therefore inspire us to create metaphoric equivalents in the workplace. The examples are associated with migration, and only for that time of the year when a difficult task needs to be achieved. At other times, smaller flocks of birds dissipate to find their own feeding grounds. The bad news for humans is that teamwork is not instinctive and needs to be nurtured and encouraged. One example from my own team was implementing a Monday call that all team members across Europe, India, and USA were invited to attend. It was voluntary, would last no longer than one hour, and was an opportunity for teams and individuals to update their colleagues and myself on weekly progress and requests for support. The call was for the benefit of the team to learn and offer help to one another. I usually opened the call and listened to each person in turn. I invited other team leaders to chair the call every few weeks to rotate the lead. The call was open to any other functions with a stake in our progress to listen to the team for their own needs in supporting collective success. If any person or business unit wanted to know what was happening in my team, I just invited them to join the Monday call to listen. Any required follow up could be done after the call. Thus, we flew together every week for an hour. Outside that time, each individual or team was free to interact with colleagues as they saw fit. Any requirement for more information was encouraged to be met outside the Monday call. Every six months or so, I would ask if the team was still getting value from the Monday call, and it prevailed for over ten years.

In business, I experienced an annual abmigration with an equivalent challenge to a five thousand-mile bird migration during the corporate annual planning cycle. This was at the time of the close of one financial year and the beginning of the next. The planning process lasts two months or more, requiring teams from across the world to submit their plans and proposed targets for the upcoming financial year. Once the individual team plans are agreed by me, they are aggregated for a consolidated submission to head office. This annual planning cycle is common in all large businesses. During this time, we fly together, and total transparency is the order of the day. I insist that submissions are shared with colleagues so that each person's and team's targets are declared to each other. This facilitates a discussion on where further opportunities for growth might come from, particularly with emerging technologies like the Internet of Things (IOT), automation, and all things digital. We start our annual planning process a few weeks before the head office requests to be ahead of the game, and we ensure that our bottom-up planning has the highest chance of prevailing. One thing I learnt from this annual 'migration' was that bottom-up plans produced greater challenges than top-down, provided there was total transparency with the team members. I am not sure why this happened, but it did, year after year. I speculated that the flock chose to fly higher due to the psyche of fuelled ambition and competition within the various teams. Indeed, on some occasions, I had to remind some of my team members of the story about Icarus from Greek mythology. Daedalus, the father of Icarus, had made artificial wings for them to flee from Crete. He asked his son not to fly too low or too high so that the sea's dampness would not clog his wings or the sun's heat melt them. Icarus ignored his father's instruction as he flew too close to the sun. The wax in his wings melted, and he perished into the sea. The story is a good metaphor for annual planning exercises!

This section has been about animal instincts as a way of identifying the influences on our lives and how to recognise them, cope with them, and use them to assist in our liberation. These influences will manifest in your PSP and will be on show to others.

Liberation summary:

- Realise the limits of your tethered thinking and appreciate that those different from you increase your breadth of thinking.
- Develop improvements in your team's performance and distinguish them from genuine innovation.
- Find the innovators and bring them to the table; the wackier, the better! These are likely to be younger team members
- Look in the mirror regularly to see how many monkeys are on your back.
- Become proficient in developing a forest to nurture the good monkeys.
- Get rid of the bad monkeys by giving them to someone else or taming them.
- Avoid becoming a dinosaur by fully embracing change and transformation. Enthuse and encourage others to do the same.
- When in doubt, promote pace over precision as the best means of implementing change.
- Commit to flying together in formation with your team and extended team to produce differentiated performance. Flying together is the most efficient way of tackling large issues.
- Treat major initiatives like birds migrating. Don't be afraid to rotate your position from time to time, and don't fly too near the sun or the sea.

- Be aware that your PSP is impacted by the animal instincts mentioned in this chapter.

Liberation from worrying too much and negativity

As a manager in my early years, I was consumed with self-doubt and worried a great deal. I bit my nails and even took to smoking cigarettes. I was often promoted earlier than my colleagues and was among the youngest ever promoted to branch manager, marketing manager, executive positions, and the like. So, my performance must have been acceptable and my presence and behaviour must have been satisfactory, but at what cost to my well being! I eventually discovered that worry and negativity can be managed and that therein lies liberation and an improved PSP.

We all worry; it is natural. We worry about our personal life and work. At times, it becomes all consuming and clouds our judgement and thinking and threatens our self-esteem. It is impossible to eradicate our propensity to worry, but it can be put in perspective and be boxed in to some extent.

I once recall someone of considerable business experience saying to me, 'There are only two things to worry about. Those things you control and those things you cannot control. For the second, stop worrying because you can do nothing about it. For the first, stop worrying and start acting on reducing or eliminating the cause of worry.' This was sound advice indeed, but I chose to add a third category to the 'worry' list: those things that you can influence.

Whenever I inherited a new business unit, early on in my interaction with my new team, I would ask the leaders to gather with their direct reports for an unscripted planning session using a marker pen and a blank flip chart. I would introduce myself and reflect on the recent performance, good or bad, and ask the assembled team to list all the things that were preventing them from being successful or being even more successful. Invariably, the sessions started slowly. No one wanted to be the first to complain, lest they be seen as negative. Most waited for their team leaders to start. However, gradually people would pipe up with 'safe' suggestions: our pricing was high compared to the competitors, we did not invest enough in advertising, and we spent too much time on administration rather than doing our jobs. The sessions always seemed to follow a symphonic pattern: Beginning with a slow movement, building to a crescendo, and then calming to a satisfying finale.

As I wrote up what was said, I asked for no clarification and did not challenge any ideas in order to indicate that no point was too trivial or unworthy. As people saw me writing, the momentum gathered, and more individuals in the room became confident to shout out their point. I furiously tried to keep up, turning page after page and writing. Eventually, the substantive concerns started to appear like 'our leadership is weak', 'our contracting process puts customers off before we even start', and 'our production process is not fit for the purpose'. As the team realised that I was just writing and not seeking explanation or justification, the 'vomit' eventually came. In fact, I came to call these sessions 'Vomit sessions', designed to get all the 'nasties' out onto the flip chart. The vomit, in fact, holds the real issues that people are reluctant to volunteer for fear of reprisal.

The sessions were cathartic for everyone. As the vomit dried to a trickle, I would say, 'surely there must be more things that are wrong'. Paraphrasing that question a few times would eventually exhaust all the points. I then went back to the beginning and read out each point from the beginning.

'So the things that are preventing us from being more successful are ...' It was not uncommon to have more than ten flip chart pages covered in points. I read each one to ensure that it was captured correctly in order to invite an acknowledgement or amend the wording to clarify the point. In essence, these were the things that the team were worrying about. After reading them all out, I told them that we were going to characterise each point with one out of three labels.

- The point was under our control (C).
- The point was not under our control, but we could influence the people who controlled it (I).
- The point was something we could neither control or influence (N).

As we went back to the beginning, each point was read out and assigned a C, I, or N. This time there would generally be some discussion to better understand the point before classifying it. As an example of the classification, there were points like the following:

- 'Too much time spent on administration rather than doing the job.' Clearly, this is something under our control. We can reschedule the administration to times when the job is less busy or when the customers are less available. This point would be a C.
- 'Our pricing is uncompetitive.' This is something generally done by a finance department in a

corporate head office. It cannot be controlled by the team, but the team could influence a change by, say, providing evidence of competitive pricing. This would then be marked with an I.

- 'The currency exchange rate is too high.' Now, this is definitely something that will impact profitability and competitiveness in international business but is something that can neither be controlled nor influenced by the team. This would attract an N.

Across the many such sessions that I have run in different industries, a pattern emerged that has proved consistent. Fewer than 35% of the points attract a C, 15–20% attract an I, and the majority, 50% or so, draw an N rating. In other words, teams spend much of their time worrying about things they neither control nor influence. Once this is understood and agreed upon, a whole lot of weeds are cleared from the garden. Once the classification work is completed, the individuals or teams are asked to produce action plans and allocate owners for the category C items and category I items. In my experience, these sessions proved invaluable in establishing a working relationship with new business units. Clearly, once it has been used, the teams are aware of what is coming. Nonetheless, repeating the exercise periodically reveals fewer Ns and Is. The final part of the session is to review the output and identify the points that refer to the team's inherent shortcomings. There are always very few – too few. A session that I ran in the USA with a team I inherited produced zero personal issues.

I refer to people's own shortcomings or needs that require focus to be more successful. Thus, it is very rare for the points to include things like the following:

- I do not understand my products or services well enough.
- I am not a good presenter.
- I do not spend enough time preparing for meetings or presentations.
- I do not ask for help often enough.
- I do not invite others to help me overcome my shortcomings.
- I do not plan my time well.
- I leave too much to the last minute.
- I do not spend enough time with customers.
- I do not do a very good job of galvanising a winning team.
- I am not a good motivator.

When there are very few personal shortcomings in the flip chart exercise, I conduct a similar session, but with a difference. This time, the blank flip chart is turned away from the gaze of the other team members and myself. Individuals are invited to draft the list of shortcomings that the team or the individuals have. By turning the flip chart around (away from the group), there is less embarrassment at writing and no opportunity for peer ridicule, as each person goes up when they feel they have something to write. The flip chart question is, 'The things I need to do better for us to be more successful are...?' This session invites team members to write up their personal issues when they are ready or during the session breaks in the meeting. When the writing has dried up, the flip chart can be turned around and the individual and team output discussed. Duplicates can be removed, leaving a list of things that the team needs to do to improve their performance. As each point does not have an identified owner, the discussion can be open, unless the individuals choose to reveal themselves. Invariably, the individuals and teams realise that much of the opportunity for improved success rests with themselves and that an action plan can be drawn up. In fact, it is likely that these are the things that they have been worrying about the most – their personal shortcomings and development needs.

These flip charts can be kept and referred back to from time to time. In my experience, once people get to understand the points that are neither under the team's control nor influence and assume greater personal responsibility, the list of things to worry about diminishes. Earlier, I recalled a session that I ran in the USA with a newly inherited team that was underperforming for the previous three years. This was the team that identified zero personal issues. Following the flip chart session that I ran with them, I sent a paper copy of their session and referred to it regularly when I met the individual members of the team and when I met the team leaders. It took some three months for them to 'get' the idea that they were largely responsible for their own performance and that excuses and blaming others were no longer accepted. They also realised that they would be supported in taking risks that they had previously avoided. In the following two financial years, the USA team grew their business by 42% and 40% respectively. One could reasonably argue that the difference in performance was directly linked with a greater freedom from worry and understanding and increasing their sphere of control.

A poignant example on liberation from worrying comes from a film called *Bridge of Spies*, starring Tom Hanks and Mark Rylance, released in 2015. The film is set in the time of the late 1950s and early 1960s, when the Soviet Union and the United States of America were embroiled in espionage during the so-called Cold War. Mark Rylance plays Rudolph Abel, a real-life character. In 1957, for his involvement in what became known as the Hollow Nickel Case (a reference to where the CIA found secret coded messages in a small coin), the US court in New York convicted Abel on three counts of conspiracy as a Soviet spy and sentenced him to 30 years of imprisonment. He served just over four years of his sentence before he was exchanged for an American U-2 pilot, who had been captured in the Soviet Union.

In the movie, Tom Hanks plays the part of James B Donovan, a real-life lawyer assigned to defend Abel as required by US law, despite the institutionalised hatred for Soviet spies at the time. Donovan and Abel develop a personal relationship that evolves throughout the movie. Abel (Rylance) is a very cool customer who is rarely phased by any of the events, including the threat of execution. During the movie, Donovan (Hanks), on three occasions, draws attention to Abel's lack of worry. On the first occasion, when Abel is threatened with execution as a spy at his trial, Donovan remarks, 'you don't seem alarmed', to which Abel replies 'would it help?' Later, when the Soviets disown Abel after his conviction, Donovan asks, 'do you never worry?', to which Abel replies, 'would it help?' Finally, when in Berlin to effect the exchange for the American U-2 pilot on a bridge, the exchange is delayed as the Soviets do not arrive on time. During the delay, Donovan asks Abel what he expects to happen to him when he returns to Russia. Abel says, 'You mean that my people might shoot me?' Donovan asks once again 'Are you not worried?' To which, for the third time, Abel asks, 'would it help?'. This is a good question for us all to reflect on.

Another important aspect on worry is about what happens at the end of the day as one retires to sleep. As a preamble to the consideration of worry and sleep, I offered coaching and mentoring sessions for my team members, but not at bedtime! I had offered these one-to-one sessions on the basis that it was private and that no notes would be taken and no reference would be made to the discussions in business hours. It was a voluntary scheme; so, the individual needed to request the meetings and could stop them at any time.

I had previously been trained in coaching and mentoring and was a committee member of the UK government's Partners in Leadership programme for Head Teachers, as stated earlier. The idea was that Head Teachers, in fact, ran a business and rarely taught their pupils. Thus, senior business people were chosen to provide business awareness coaching for local Head Teachers to help them run and develop their school and staff.

Thus, there was some practical experience that I could offer to my team. On one occasion, I met with Raja, and the discussion was entirely about his not being able to sleep. I witnessed this as over some time, I had read emails that were written by Raja at 2 am, 3 am, and other times during the night. It was a source of great frustration to Raja and his family. I asked him why he did this. His answer was that he could not go to sleep until he had cleared his mental in-tray of worries and things that needed doing. I could relate to this, as my wife had a similar tendency to talk about matters of the day and ask questions before she was able to sleep. After the session, I looked up some postings on pre-sleep anxiety. A comment read as follows:

'When you go to sleep, since your body is not doing anything anymore, it is normal for your brain activity to increase. You think about what you've done today, which makes you think about a thousand other stuff that happened in your whole life, you can call it a "stream of consciousness". I guess we should see it as something pretty awesome that our brain does.'

I guess it can be pretty awesome, if you can sleep! It also turned out that Raja was a perfectionist. His desk was always laid out in a particular pattern, with each item in its place. He would straighten papers and move them a few millimetres so that they were in the right place. I am not sure that contributed to sleeplessness, but I am certain that his perfectionist nature was material to his sleep anxiety.

When reflecting on my own experiences, I had no trouble sleeping on most nights. Following the coaching session with Raja, I rationalised that I probably had a mental in-tray that was equal to Raja's and my wife's but could somehow put it aside until the morning. I called this activity 'turning the page'. If the thoughts and list of things to do are imagined to be written down on a page, then the trick is to turn to the next blank page before sleeping and then turn back to the list again in the morning. I shared this thought, and it did seem to help

Raja. We discussed the concept, and he agreed that he did have a mental list that he went through before sleeping. Over the next few weeks, I asked him how the nightly page turning was going. Easier said than done, I was told, but the nocturnal emails gradually diminished. When my wife also starts discussing her list, I now say, 'please just turn the page and we can talk in the morning'. It is not guaranteed to work but is offered as an idea to help people to stop worrying, especially when you are in bed and can do absolutely nothing about anything!

The final thought on worry is what I call Should've, Would've, Could've (SWC). These are the things that you regret doing or saying. By definition, they are in the past, and one thing I have learnt above all else is that you cannot change the past. However, we all worry about things that we did or said and wished we hadn't. There is no magical answer here. The things that have helped me are saying 'sorry' to people whom I have offended, and where possible, rectifying the mistakes. So, instead of worrying about them, develop an action plan for rectification. If it is too late, then be free to admit your mistake to whomsoever, but first to yourself. Anyway, if you conduct the flip chart session described at the beginning of this chapter, all the items of 'should've, would've, could've' would be marked with an 'N' as you can neither control or influence the past.

Be assured that your PSP will be impacted by the way you respond to things that are the cause of worry. Your presence in particular. Have you noticed that some people never seem to worry? I am sure they do, like the rest of us, but their presence exudes calmness and assuredness. Abel in *Bridge of Spies* is a case in point.

In summary, there are only three types of things to worry about: those things you control, those things you can influence, and those things you can neither control nor influence. Spend no time on the latter, as this is the shortcut to high blood pressure, and take action rather than worry about the former two, especially the things under your control. And that includes yourself. As worry takes hold as it inevitably will, ask yourself, like Abel, would it help? If you worry too much before sleeping, turn to a blank page at bedtime. For those things that you regret from the past (SWC's), produce an action plan for them only if they can be revisited.

Negativity

Negativity plays a large part in all our lives, and not the least from within. Self-doubt and a fear of failure is a normal state of affairs in most of us. We all have that inner voice or alter ego that likes to take us down – telling ourselves that we cannot do certain things, or ideas will not work, and persuading us that we do not possess the internal capability and resources to achieve our goals. The negative inner voice's job description is to diminish your Personal Share Price. The alter ego cannot be ignored, but it can be sidelined through constructive thinking. Recognising that negativity exists and trying to give it less credibility by continuing to achieve life goals is itself liberating. We can develop an 'I told you so' response to the alter ego before it uses it on us! As a sports coach once told me, there is no such thing as failure, only unintended outcomes.

There are several works on the subject of the alter ego from professional psychologists who are qualified on this subject. For example, Psychologytoday.com states that 'with time, a bit of elbow grease and an understanding of your own character strengths, you can become friendlier, more caring and less stressed by life'. However, I am no psychologist, so the 'inside negativity' will not be further explored here except to acknowledge its presence.

I am more concerned with the elements of external negativity and the strategies that have worked for me.

The good leave

It is possible to be agitated or infuriated by the smallest of things, even a single gesture. A relative once visited our house and looked around at our rooms, pictures, artefacts, and décor, and then, with a single gesture, sent my wife into a rage. The aunt simply wiped her middle finger across the top of a piece of furniture, and rubbed her thumb and finger together, and then wiped her hand with a tissue. The message was clear. Your house is not clean! It was a powerful gesture intended to rile, and it did. There is a joke about relatives coming to stay for Christmas, and how in a few days you cannot wait for them to leave. So even loved ones press the destruct button and create a climate of negativity sooner or later.

Over the years, I witnessed my wife doing everything possible to please my mother, but sooner or later, the mother-in-law jokes invariably became a reality. However, things became much better between them when I was sitting watching a cricket match on TV with my wife. I heard the commentator say about a wickedly good ball, 'that was a good leave'. In other words, the batsman was better off to leave the ball rather than attempt to hit it. The 'good leave' was because the commentator knew that to attempt to hit the wickedly good ball carried a high risk of being caught out by a fielder. It then struck me – the same idea should apply to wicked comments from people, which are designed to provoke. Just leave them. Do not attempt to ask for clarification, or worse still, try to respond to the point (hit the ball) as this will inevitably achieve its aim to provoke, and you may be caught out!

My wife and I now joke about the 'good leave', and domestic harmony took a definite upturn. Now if the aunt wipes our furniture or my mother makes a barbed comment, my wife says absolutely nothing. The bad news is that you cannot leave every ball, so the trick is to leave the ones that are most designed to provoke and thus frustrate the bowler.

In business, the 'good leave' is equally valuable when used correctly. It is the silent equivalent of 'no comment' but much more powerful. Here I do distinguish between ignoring someone and a 'good leave'. Ignoring someone creates its own negativity, but a 'good leave' maintains connection in a constructive way – a test between bowling and batting skills that both sportsmen should enjoy. However, you cannot leave every ball, and choosing the ones to leave is a test of skill for a batsman and a manager.

So, be aware when questions or points are designed to provoke, and be ready to hit a bad ball for a six, i.e. for a point that you have the answers and facts for, but be equally proud of a 'good leave' when appropriate. Practicing the skill will improve the positivity in interactions with friends, family, and colleagues.

With those not familiar with the game of cricket, I am sure other sporting analogies apply, for instance, in tennis and volleyball leaving a ball because it will be out of court rather than trying to return it can be considered a 'good leave' as it wins the point by doing nothing.

The questioner controls the conversation:

Questions are, in my experience, the most powerful way of creating and maintaining a positive atmosphere. Again, it will take practice to perfect, but it pays huge dividends in the foundation of positive dialogue.

The premise is that we are all given to write and talk in statements. This is fine until the statements create a negative environment. I am sure we have all heard colleagues bad mouth other colleagues – 'she is no good at her job.' A statement that requires no facts has a trap. To agree or disagree takes you in a clear direction of support ('I agree') or potential conflict ('I do not agree').

Of course, this type of comment might be a great example of a 'good leave', merely not to respond. But it is usually designed to provoke a response. This is where a question is beneficial. 'What is it that you think she could do to improve?' or, even better, 'what is it that *we* could do to help her improve?'

Questions make it almost impossible to create an atmosphere of conflict. Questions work extremely well when faced with an air of potential negativity, usually recognised in criticism. One response I like and have used many times is when a team member criticises some element of the company's offerings – criticisms like the lack of product features, the lack of management commitment, the lack of competitive pricing, the lack of delivery resources, and so on. I listen attentively; this is vital to show engagement and interest. The criticism could go on for a few minutes. At a pause, I ask if that is all. Sometimes, this is taken as encouragement to continue! When the retching has ended, I ask the person, 'if we were to fix these things, how much extra target would you be willing to take?' This works pretty much every time. The premise for the complaint is that the original business plan or target had assumed perfection for all aspects of business, that products are perfect, competitors are inferior, and customers are clear on what the differentiators are. The complaint is invariably designed to hide any shortcomings of the individuals' performance. I find that successful people rarely complain.

But the question should not be a smart response to someone who is clearly frustrated either with themselves or their products, services, business potential, or whatever. The question, therefore, needs to be set in the context of a caring response. 'It is great that you care enough to tell me of your deep concerns, but if we were to fix, say one element, which would you recommend we fix first?' Depending on the response, a further question might be 'and if we were to do that, what extra business could we get?'

The more common response I have witnessed to such vitriol from a team member is for the managers to counter the assertions with rat-a-tat facts to refute the point. This creates an 'I win, you lose' environment from which the opportunity and ownership for improved business evaporate, and a basis for conflict is created. In the worst case, people give up coming forward with frustrations that may have opportunities for the future benefit buried within them. I have heard people say – no good talking to X, he never listens, or he always puts me down. My advice is not to stifle the airing of frustrations, but to look for the gold nuggets in the frustrations through attentive listening and by using questions.

Much can be learnt from TV and Radio interviewers. They are trained to ask closed questions to invite a yes or no response from business leaders and politicians. By the same token, politicians, in particular, are trained to ignore the question and repeat policy; but that's another story. The difference between open and closed questions is important to understand in the journey of liberation from negativity. In talking to children, the point is very obvious. When asking a closed question of a child, a 'yes' or 'no' response will be followed by nothing. This can become very frustrating as conversation never materialises. By contrast, asking open questions will provide at least some chance of dialogue. Try using open and closed questions at home and see the effect. 'Have you done your homework?' becomes 'what homework did you have and how did you get on with it?' The first question is a closed question, answered with a yes or no. The latter question is open and invites a conversation.

It is very difficult to create an atmosphere of negativity when using open questions. Open questions (what, where, how, when) always create an opportunity for dialogue. During a dialogue, frustrations usually diminish, and the likelihood of a positive aura increases.

A further development from open questions is what Nancy Kline has trademarked as Incisive Questions to one's self. Nancy is president of *Time to Think*, an international coaching and leadership development company. Nancy contends that assumptions drive our thinking, feelings, decision making, and action. The good ideas and feelings come from true, liberating assumptions. The bad ones come from untrue, limiting assumptions. So, to break through from bad to good, the mind seems to go through roughly this sequence of questions: 1. What am I assuming that is limiting my thinking here? 2. What am I assuming that is most limiting my thinking here? 3. Is that assumption true? 4. What is a liberating, true alternative to the limiting assumption? 5. If I knew (insert true alternative), what would I think or feel or do? Thus, Nancy Kline proposes a means of controlling the conversation with ourselves by asking four open questions and one closed question. I suggest that the ratio of four open questions to one closed is relevant in creating positive dialogue. Thus, to limit negativity in interactions, always search for open questions. The consequential dialogue will most often be positive in its outcome.

Three words to hate and three to love

In an earlier chapter, I proffered that almost everyone is better than they think they are. We tend to put our own limitations on what can be achieved. It is very disheartening for discussions on improved performance or added value or brainstorming to be hit with a barrage of negativity − 'that won't work', 'we don't have the resources, skills or money to do something like that', 'Head Office will never agree', etc.

Even in early childhood, the limitations of our potential become influenced by negativity and the tethered thinking mentioned earlier − 'I'm no good at painting', 'I'm no good at sports', and the like. If not recognised and treated, these early signs of limitation become mature cancers in later life. I became aware that I was irritated more and more when these negative waves hit me, especially early on in a discussion.

So the three words that I began to hate were 'I can't because'. It still drives me nuts when I hear them or their derivatives. The reason they are used in general is to avoid doing work. Past failures build a lexicon of excuses to be used at any future point that looks similar in nature. But these past failures are opportunities for learning. No one minds people making mistakes; the crime is in repeating them or not learning from them. A prominent and very successful businessman, Sir John Harvey-Jones, once said that provided he made one more good decision than bad, he was content.

And so, I arrived at the three words I love, 'I can if'. This response suggests that all things are possible depending on the 'if' − if I have appropriate funding, if I can get the people I need, if the company invests in the idea. I became more aware of and sensitive to the two sets of three words, and my antennae are now permanently attuned.

These two sets of words are very simple and unambiguous. Once you become sensitive to the two sets of words, it becomes easier to steer conversations. The 'because' in the first set of words can be explored to see if there is a justifiable reason for not doing what has been asked. Clearly, if the reasons for not doing something can be resolved, then an 'I can't because' response can be transformed into an 'I can if'. The conversation becomes 'So if your issue can be resolved, then you are happy to proceed'.

If you share my hatred and liking for the two sets of words, share the thought with your team. In my experience, once people know about the sensitivity, 'I can't because', or similar expressions become a rare occurrence. Coming back to an earlier section on why the Indian people are so given to answering 'yes' to every closed question, they are most of the time subliminally bypassing an 'I can if' with just a shortcut of 'yes'. This is one reason why I like them so much.

For the final comment on the two sets of three words, I again turn to the media. In Britain, each year for the past seven years there has been a top-rated TV reality programme called 'The Great British Bake-Off.' It has become a surprisingly popular show, attracting the largest TV audience for the 2015 and 2016 series. The format involves a number of volunteer contestants baking recipes according to different themes. Every week of the series, a new theme is revealed, which the contestants need to interpret in their baked item. Each bake has a time limit, and the contestants are encouraged to use their own creative ideas to produce a bake that tastes good, looks good, and matches the theme of the week. There is a succession of elimination rounds ending in the last week with three finalists from which a winner is chosen.

In October 2015, the competition was won by a 30-year-old woman by the name of Nadiya Hussain. She had started the competition lacking in confidence. Yet, she improved each week and eventually made the final. When she won the contest, she could not believe it. In the final interview, with a tearful eye, she said something that was extremely powerful:

'I am never, ever going to put boundaries on myself, ever again. I'm never going to say I don't think I can... I can and I will'.

So, Nadiya had, in fact, come from the 'I can't because' to 'I can if' state of mind during the programme series and ended up as the winner. Nadiya Hussain's words should often be read, especially when tempted into an 'I can't because' scenario. Interestingly, Nadiya went on to become a household name, wrote her own best-selling recipe book, and became a TV personality. In 2017, she even announced that she would host her own TV programme. An incredible result from just turning from 'I can't because' to 'I can if'. Imagine what happened to her Personal Share Price from the beginning of the programme to her success and beyond. The 'I can if' attitude will doubtless improve the PSP.

.

Liberation summary:

- Classify the things that you worry about into those things that you can control (C) and take action, those things that you influence (I) and take action, and those things that you can neither control nor influence (N) and dismiss them.
- Run a flip chart session with your team on what is preventing further success. Wait for the 'vomit', write and do not challenge. Run a similar session for the improvements required for the team and individuals. This is what they are really worrying about – their own shortcomings.
- Become a facilitator, coach, and mentor for individuals to help them develop. You may need formal training in this... which is within you control!
- When worrying gets the better of you, think Bridge of Spies and 'would it help?'
- When worrying before sleep, imagine the worry list written down on a page and turn to a blank page. You can turn back in the morning!
- Classify the Should've, Would've, Could've (SWC) worries with an 'N'. Bank the learning and dismiss them.
- When the alter ego says that you cannot do certain things, find liberation by achieving your goals and saying 'I told you so' first!
- When someone is trying to rile you, think about 'the good leave' to diffuse the situation.
- Use questions as a means of taming negativity. Use open questions in preference to closed questions.

- Be aware of 'I can't because' mindsets and create an environment in your team for 'I can if'. Think Nadiya Hussain.
- Monitor the impact of managing worry and negativity on your PSP.

Liberation from risky hiring

I was once told that first-class people recruit first-class people, while second-class people recruit third-class people. Although the statement is somewhat trivial, it does serve to remind us that hiring is a risky business for both candidates and interviewers.

One of the aspects that will impact longer-term performance is being able to hire the right people and avoid 'bad apples'. Your PSP will be adversely impacted by poor hiring as poor hires undoubtedly manifest in poor performance. Job interviews typically last an hour to 90 minutes and even when a few people have interviewed the same person, the combined experience will be less than 4–5 hours in total. By contrast, once hired, the impact will last years in most cases. Very occasionally, a candidate is so poor that summary dismissal can be justified in the short term, but that just means starting again! It also entails an admission that the process for hiring was wholly inadequate.

Throughout my career, I have worked primarily in business leadership roles. During this time, I have attended numerous training courses, including those on interview techniques. However, even with this knowledge, I felt that each hire was something of a risk for both sides. If a hire does not work out, it is wrong for both parties, not just one. Furthermore, the interviewing process is choreographed to some extent, in that candidates are advised on how to make a favourable impression at interviews. There are over 13 million artefacts on Google for 'job interview tips' or 'how to create a good impression at a job interview'. Similarly, questions for candidates too often follow a standard format, and therefore, responses can be rehearsed. One could argue that it is, therefore, something of a game. The trick to reducing the risk in hiring is to create a methodology that is new to candidates and therefore cannot be rehearsed and involves them in self-certification.

From interviewing experiences and training, I developed an interview process that has served me well. What surprised me is that the interviewees frequently remarked that they had not experienced a similar process and had quite enjoyed it. Moreover, when more than one of us interviewed the same person, I was able to find material evidence and candidate experience that my colleagues had not picked up. When my Human Resources (HR) colleagues sat in on interviews, they too commented on how the process provided relevant information in a relatively short time that gave deeper insight into the candidates' skills and experience. Praise from the HR is praise indeed.

In some cases, even though the candidate had been pre-vetted by the HR, the process I developed was able to uncover facts that indicated the unsuitability of the candidate for the role in question. It seemed, therefore, that I may have evolved a technique that had merit and reduced the risk of hiring for both sides. I called this the Sums process, which becomes clear later.

Preamble to the Sums process

A Curriculum Vitae (CV) is the common starting point for all interviews. We have all written one, and they are, not unnaturally, a flattering interpretation of experience, education, and performance. However, it is what is missing, misrepresented, or misinterpreted that might be the clue to whether it is a good hire or not. I repeat, a bad hire is not right for the company or the individual, so, it is in everyone's interest to get it right.

From the CV, a few notes should be taken and an attempt made to find something in common with the candidate. The knowledge of a school, university, or company that they had worked at, possible mutual people connects, shared extramural activities, and the like. Or, in some cases, perhaps noticing an unusual element of past work. Thus, when the candidate arrives, it is important to demonstrate that you have read the CV. An opening remark highlighting the item that you have chosen will confirm any doubts about you having read the CV and create a more relaxed atmosphere for the interview. Opening remarks like I 'see you went to XYZ school', or 'it appears you are a keen golfer', 'did you come across Mr X when you worked at the ABC company' all help put the candidate at ease and act as an icebreaker.

I remember seeing an episode of The Office sitcom on television. (The Office was a very popular TV series that mocked the going-ons in a typical office). In this episode, the office manager, played by Ricky Gervais, reviews a huge pile of CVs on his desk. Without reading them, he puts half of the CVs in the bin saying, 'I don't hire unlucky people!' So it is important to show that you are not a Ricky Gervais character.

A final point on the CV is to show the candidate the CV you received on paper or screen and ask if they recognise it. This is because some recruitment companies edit candidate-submitted CVs before sending them. It also confirms that you have taken the trouble to read the CV as you have it in front of you. Establishing this early on is important to ensure full disclosure.

After the opening remarks and brief exchange, the interview can begin in earnest.

The first interview question I ask is 'why are you here?' and I explain that this is to check that what I have been told is the same as what the candidate has been told. Even this question can be disarming, but you want to know that the candidate is clear about the type of role that they are applying for. In more than one case, the interviewee faulted at this first question with replies like 'Well, I was told that you were looking for people' or 'I was told your company pays well'. Not a good start, and interviews can be cut short by perhaps sympathetically saying, 'I am not sure we are the right company for you'. In other instances, the candidate has been misled by the recruitment company that they have been working with. By not understanding the finer points of a candidate's previous experience, the suitability for a particular role can be poor. For example, in IT services, the distinction between applications development experience and infrastructure services is material, but both can be described as IT services experience. Be aware that some recruitment firms have incentives for the number of interviews conducted, and not just for the confirmed hires.

At this point, the foundation for the interview should be firm, and the Sums process can begin.

The Sums process

We now come to the meat of a process that I developed over many interviews. It requires the candidate to do some sums, as I put it, simple sums. A series of A + B + C = 100 sums. The A, B, and C are changed as relevant to the job requirements. The intention is to pay attention to the three most important aspects of a particular role, and the three most important attributes of each aspect (A, B, and C). Thus the sums become as follows:

	Attributes
Aspect 1	A + B + C = 100
Aspect 2	A + B + C = 100
Aspect 3	A + B + C = 100

The total of 100 represents the individual's total experience of each aspect, based on the scoring that the candidate gives for each A, B, and C attributes. Note that the split across A + B + C needs to add to 100. Sometimes, candidates struggle with this!

The interviewer writes all the sums on a piece of paper, as well as the aspects, attributes, and a total of 100, leaving brackets underneath the attributes of each equation. The important part is that it is the candidate that needs to fill in the number in the brackets, and not the interviewer. I explain that the idea of each A + B + C = 100 is intended to put a relative measure to the experience that the candidate has across the three main attributes of each given aspect. To check for understanding at this point, which is crucial, a non-relevant example is used. I generally use an experience in sport as the example.

The attributes A, B, and C represent well-known sports, say Football = A, Athletics = B, and Tennis = C. The candidate is then given a sheet of paper to record their relative sports experiences either as participants or spectators. The candidate then completes the sum as follows:

Aspect: Experience in three major sports (as spectator or participant). Attributes A, B, and C are the following:

```
    A     +    B     +     C
(Football)  (Athletics)  (Tennis)
   [    ]  + [    ]  + [    ]  = 100
```

The candidate then fills in the blanks. At this stage, they may ask questions for clarification, but the candidate should be encouraged to interpret it as they understand it. It will be discussed when all the sums are complete, as that will reflect the total candidate experience examined by the sums. In any event, the sum is a relative experience of the candidate; so, provided that their understanding of the attributes is consistent, the detail does not matter.

The candidate may then complete as follows:

```
  A    +    B    +    C

[ 75 ] + [ 10 ] + [  15  ] = 100
```

You can then interpret that the candidate has the most experience with football, which is way ahead of athletics and tennis, according to their own relative scoring. A conversation can then take place on the story behind the marking. 'What was the thinking behind putting 10 against athletics? Why did you score football so much higher than athletics or tennis?' The chances are that the candidate played football, was very keen on the sport, and may have been a coach. The relevance of the scoring is that the spread of the candidate's scores reveals insights that can be explored and discussed for greater understanding.

This part of the exercise is to check understanding and is worth spending some time on, for the remainder of the A, B, C sums are related to the specific role that the candidate is being interviewed for.

I ask the candidate to complete three sets of role-related sums before they are all discussed. Again, any attempt for clarification of the points should be responded to with 'whatever you think it means', since it is their relative score that is important.

As a real example, I have recruited for sales roles in selling IT software services to existing and prospective financial services customers. In this case, the first aspect is sales experience. The three attributes A, B, and C represent the major activities in the lifecycle of the sales process. The relevant experience is, therefore, spread across the following:

A = Customer sales (selling the IT services to a customer account)
B = Solutioning (designing a solution that fits the client's needs)
C = Delivery (delivering the IT services' solution)

The first sum for **Sales Experience** then becomes the following:

$$A \quad + \quad B \quad + \quad C$$
(Sales) (Solutioning) (Delivery)
[   ] + [   ] + [   ] = 100
(sales cycle experience)

From the relative scores, you can determine where in the sales cycle the candidate has the most experience in dealing with customers. Here, one potential pitfall can be avoided. I have witnessed a number of solutioning- and delivery-oriented people wanting to move into sales as it 'seems more fun' or 'pays better', but if the experience is not in sales per se, the risks are clear.

The second A, B, and C attributes concern the aspect of financial services **Industry Experience**. In financial services, the main industry attributes are banking, insurance, and capital markets.

```
        A          +     B     +      C
    (Banking)        (Insurance)   (Capital Markets)
      [      ]   +    [     ]  +    [      ] = 100
(financial services industry experience)
```

The relative scores here can identify which lines of business the candidate has the most experience in. Someone experienced in insurance would represent a risk if the required role were to sell to capital markets' clients, however generically the candidate is experienced in financial services. The relative split will identify potential risks for discussion.

The final A, B, and C is an evaluation of the aspect of **IT Services Experience**. The three main service lines (attributes) in IT services are all things to do with software (Applications)= A, IT Infrastructure (hardware, networks, storage, etc.) = B, or IT operations called Business Process Outsourcing (BPO) = C.

```
        A        +       B      +      C
  (Applications)    (Infrastructure)   (BPO)
     [     ]    +     [     ]   +    [   ] = 100
```

In a few cases this has identified BPO-experienced people applying for application sales roles or vice versa. Both represent experience in IT services but require significantly different skills. As a reminder, the numbers in the equation are completed by the candidate; so, it is their numbers, and, therefore, their representation of themselves.

Using this technique, the interviewer can play back what the candidate scoring profile reveals. The following is an example:

The role is to hire a suitable candidate for a sales role of selling IT application services to banks.

Sales Experience

A	+	B	+	C
(Sales)		(Solutioning)		(Delivery)
[70]	+	[20] +		[10] = 100

Industry Experience

A	+	B	+	C
(Banking)		(Insurance)		(Capital Markets)
[70]	+	[30] +		[0] = 100

IT Services Experience

A	+	B	+	C
(Applications)		(Infrastructure)		(BPO)
[60]	+	[10]	+	[30] = 100

From these scores, the candidate can be asked to respond to a summary as follows:

Sales Experience

The candidate is experienced in sales (70/100 rating) but understands that solutioning (20) and delivery (10) are needed to ensure success. The candidate clearly expects other roles to be responsible for service delivery and also does not assume complete responsibility for designing the solution. This person is clearly a sales person who knows that teamwork with pre-sales and delivery people is required to ensure customer satisfaction. A discussion on the won and lost sales can follow to provide evidence to justify the profile scores.

Industry Experience

The candidate is very experienced in banking (70/100) and has significant insurance experience (30/100), but no capital markets experience. Clearly, there is no expectation that a role in capital markets will be suitable. A discussion on banking and insurance would be worthwhile regarding what is behind the candidate scoring and why banking is the dominant experience, more than twice the score for insurance. This profile matches well with the role in question.

IT Services Experience

The candidate is mostly experienced in selling applications (software) 60/100 and has some BPO experience (30/100), but little experience in infrastructure services. Thus, a role in selling infrastructure services would be unsuitable. However, all three are generic IT services capabilities. This may not have come out so clearly otherwise. As BPO and software sales are very different, it would be good to know what examples the candidate has on each of these two attributes.

The candidate can then be asked to verify whether the interviewer's summary of the relative scores is correct or not. This can also lead to a discussion on why each number was selected and insights on the relative scoring. If the candidate is experienced in selling (as in this example), a third sum can be done. This time there are only two attributes, represented as A + B = 100 (no C category). This is because there are only two major types of sales roles: Hunters and Farmers. This is important, as there is a significant difference between salespeople who are good at developing customer accounts (Farmers) and those who are adept at selling to acquire new customers (Hunters). Assume that the candidate completes the following scores:

A	+	B	
Hunting		Farming	
[70]	+	[30]	= 100

From the candidate's numbers, it is clear that more experience has been in gaining new customers (a rarer skill) than developing existing clients. As Hunters and Farmers are very different roles with very different motivations, this is important to establish and worthy of discussion. The scoring profile may also indicate that developing the customer account is also important to the candidate (30/100) rather than making the initial sale and quickly moving on.

In a previous chapter, Liberation from your cultural heritage, the importance of working with different cultures has been highlighted. If this is an important part of the role that the candidate is applying for, I ask the candidate to rate themselves on a scale of 0–100 on 'cultural diversity' experience. This need not be work related. The person may have married someone from a different culture, or may have been born or lived abroad, or worked overseas. Short term holidays of two weeks abroad do not qualify. To continue the point about using the candidate's numbers, I ask them to put an 'X' with a number on a horizontal line that represents cultural difference experience between 0–100. Zero is little cultural diversity experience, and 100 is considerable cultural diversity experience.

0---100

Before they put the cross on the line, a little more explanation may be needed. I usually say that if one was born in Yorkshire, grew up there, went to school and university there, married a local and lived there, the mark would tend to be zero. By contrast, if one was born abroad, schooled in a foreign country, married a person from another religion or creed, and worked overseas for an extended period, then the 'X' would tend well towards 100.

Example: 0---------------------------------X----------------100
                                                          65

Once they have put their mark and the corresponding number, a dialogue on why the mark was placed at the particular point can reveal more insights into the candidate's attitude and experience with cultural diversity.

The final set of numbers, written by the candidate, concern their performance over the past three years against their primary objectives in their current role. The objectives are sometimes called Key Performance Parameters (KPP) or Key Performance Indicators (KPI) or simply Objectives. There is usually more than one, and each is normally weighted. The one with the highest weighting is what needs to be known. For a sales role, continuing with the example, the highest weighted objective is normally revenue generated.

The candidate should be asked what their three most important KPPs were called in their current or last role. These need to be named by the candidate. From the three offered, the candidate should be asked what the weighting was for each. This will identify the single most important KPP as the highest weighted (KPP#1).

The final set of numbers deal with each of the last three years, measuring KPP#1 target against actual performance, as follows:

Target objective (T) versus Actual performance (A), where Year 0 is the last full year of performance, followed by the two prior years.

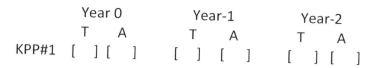

	Year 0		Year-1		Year-2	
	T	A	T	A	T	A
KPP#1	[ ]	[ ]	[ ]	[ ]	[ ]	[ ]

The targets should be numeric (measurable), and the actual performance should be either a value or percentage. Again, the numbers must be completed by the candidate. I once interviewed a candidate who did not have numerical targets, only subjective targets, and this was the point at which the interview terminated! It is not unusual for the candidate to think for some time before completing each year. Your judgement will be to see if the numbers come quickly and clearly to mind or not. This part of the process will also highlight any changes in KPP#1 over the previous three years. A change in a role within a company or between companies may come to light, which in itself is worthy of discussion. These final sets of scorings reveal a track record of performance over the last three years, from which over- and under-target performance can be discussed.

This marks the completion of the Sums process. The remainder of the interview can adopt a more normal interview conversation about the preferred ways of working, best success, worst failure, and lessons from experience. Be sure to examine the behaviours that the candidate has exhibited in various challenges and scenarios in their career to date. By now, you will have some notion of their presence, but their behaviour will need to be examined. Earlier, in the chapter on PSP, it was proffered that behaviour and presence created the foundation for performance. Try to avoid the common pitfall of placing too much emphasis on the candidate's personality. To repeat the comments made earlier, definitive research by

Walter Mischel, Stanford University psychology professor, found that personality explains less than 10% of a person's behaviour. To be clear, personality is a poor predictor of performance, because people are highly adaptive and far more flexible than personality tests give them credit for. To further emphasise this point, Professor Robin Stuart-Kotze wrote a book entitled 'Performance: The Secrets of Successful Behaviour'. Thus, during interviews, focus on past performance, behaviour, and presence, not personality.

It is also necessary to find out what the candidate enjoys doing in their spare time, as being able to relax outside of work is important to recharge the batteries. These tend to be the most usual components of an interview. By using the sums and numbers, a metric-based insight will provide a greater understanding of the candidate's suitability for a particular role. Remember, the sums and numbers are the candidate's, not yours. The result of this process is that you have a written record of the candidate's own role-related profile. This is important not just to assess the candidate's suitability for the role in question, but also as a base for discussion with other colleagues who will or have interviewed the candidate. It also serves as a valuable document to send to the HR for their records.

In conclusion, I have shown how the sums and numbers process can be used in the example of someone applying for a sales role in an IT services company. However, the process is equally adaptable to other roles where the three most important aspects can be measured across the three most relevant attributes, principal KPP and past three years performance.

To illustrate the point in recruiting for a manufacturing company role, the aspects and attributes might be as follows:

Aspect: Manufacturing Process

A	+	B	+	C
(Design/Engineering)		(Production)		(Distribution)
[ ]	+	[ ]	+	[ ] = 100

Aspect: Manufacturing Type

A	+	B	+	C
(Process)		(Line)		(Bespoke)
[ ]	+	[ ]	+	[ ] = 100

Aspect: Manufacturing Scale

A	+	B	+	C
(Large)		(Medium)		(Small)
[ ]	+	[ ]	+	[ ] = 100

And KPP#1 may be manufacturing efficiency or percentage of rework and the like.

The process is extremely flexible from the aspect and attribute definitions, but the methodology should be consistent in getting candidates to score themselves. The resulting dialogue will deliver a deeper insight into the experience-based suitability of employment for a specific role. The Sums process has served me well across different businesses and over many years. The proof is in the differentiated performance that my teams have delivered and has been recorded earlier. Furthermore, through HR, peer acknowledgement, and candidates expressions, the Sums process has materially impacted my PSP with both candidates and colleagues. I was once told by an HR person that the candidates always want to join our company after I had interviewed them. She said that they invariably enjoyed the conversation and the Sums process.

Liberation summary:

- A wrong hire is wrong for both you and the candidate. You do no one a service with an unsuitable hire.
- Demonstrate that you have read a CV by reference to a specific aspect.
- Begin with 'why are you here?' to confirm that the candidate's understanding and yours are aligned.
- You need the candidate to reveal the metrics behind their CV.
- Develop competency with the Sums process – decide your own three most important aspects and related attributes for a given role.
- Ensure that the candidate understands how to complete the A, B, C sums by using a uncontroversial example (e.g. sports).
- Have the candidate fill the blanks in the sums process. Never complete it on their behalf.
- Complete all the A, B, C sums before offering a personal interpretation of what the sums indicate.
- After discussion, gain agreement on what the sums indicate and the suitability for the role in question.
- After the sums, have the candidate complete the last three years' performance against their primary objective (KPP#1).

- If relevant, ask the candidate to position their cultural diversity experience on a scale of 0–100, and have them explain why the mark and associated number are where they are.
- Conventional interview techniques need to be integrated with the Sums process to obtain a full picture from which to decide on hiring.

30-60-90 day plan towards liberation

There will never be a better time to establish a first-rate PSP through presence and behaviour (and later performance) than during the first three months of starting a new job or role. From my experience, this is a time that decides longer-term feast or famine. I contend that the activities below will ensure that you establish not only an early positive impact but also the foundation for longer-term differentiated success and a superior PSP.

There are over 2 million articles on the subject of 30-60-90 day planning on Google! Most are associated with preparation for interviews for a new job. In most interviews, the question of what you will do in your first 90 days will come up. Many of the articles pose as being the best practice, but very few appear to be created by actual managers from their direct experience. My approach is to provide a 30-60-90 day plan that I have developed and used in many different roles across different teams, different geographies, and different cultures. Furthermore, I have cross-referenced the plan with the relevant page numbers in the rest of the book to add further context. I propose that the objective of any role in today's dynamic markets is to deliver differentiated customer value (see pages 20–25). In essence, it is 'to make a difference' in an increasingly competitive world. The principal intention of the 90-day plan should be to align you and your team to an agreed framework for differentiated success.

Now, onto the first practical challenge, a 90-day plan normally covers a period of the first three months in a new role. The bad news is that in a five-day working week, there are a maximum of 60 working days in three months. If there are 60 working days in three months, then your plan should become a 20-40-60 day plan. Already a third of the time that you thought you had is gone! Thus, my plan assumes 60 working days, and not 90 days. From this realisation, a renewed sense of urgency becomes immediately apparent.

To create a firm foundation for the plan, I offer the following thoughts:

- As my mother often said, 'you only have one chance to create a first impression'. She also used to say for any new venture, 'start as you mean to go on'. My mother's wisdom has served me well.
- Avoid the temptation to fix any systemic problems in the first 60 working days, as this will take you off course.
- 60 working days is not a long time; so, value pace over precision in this period.

I categorise my suggested 20-40-60 working day plan into three phases:

- 1–20 days: Listen and learn
- 21–40 days: Understand and implement, establish a foundation Personal Share Price (PSP)
- 41–60 days: The beginning of MADness (Make A Difference) and liberation

The MADness period represents your earliest opportunity to start as you mean to go on. Crucially, it is also the beginning of your liberation as a manager. At this stage, you have begun to empower your team to take greater personal responsibility for the things under their control or influence. Importantly, this is the period when you begin to add performance to presence and behaviour to optimise your PSP (chapter 1).

Now we move to the detail of the 20-40-60 working day plan that has allowed me to make a difference.

Listen and learn (days 1 to 20)

This period will provide the factual basis for planning ahead. As, by definition, you do not know much about your new role and team, remember that you have two ears and one mouth and should use them in that proportion. This is also the period of reciprocal first impressions with your primary stakeholders. These include your boss, peer managers in your boss' business unit, customers (internal and external), and most importantly, your direct reporting managers and wider team.

If you are new to a company, there is an additional need to learn about the organisation's purpose, values, strategy, goals, and ways of working. For guidance on the difference between how a company is structured and how it functions, see page 27. To a great extent, learning about the organisation can be done outside working hours, and even before joining, by reading annual reports, news articles, press announcements, and opinions from industry analysts. This will add to what you learnt through the job application process and be further improved as a by-product through the 60-working-days plan.

The actions for the first 20 days are as follows:

1. Complete any formal induction training that your company offers.

2. Meet your direct reports individually for 30 minutes. Prior to the meeting, provide them with a common agenda for them to prepare a document covering the following:

a. the reporting managers' team and/or individual goals

b. quantified targets versus actual performance for each of the last four quarters and the last financial year

c. a photograph and brief profile of each team member with the last twelve months' performance's RAG status (Red, Amber, Green), where green is good, amber is satisfactory, and red is below expectations.

d. a summary of current activities and forecast for the next quarter and full financial year

3. Meet the boss and share the 20-40-60 working day plan. Have this formal meeting after you have met your direct reports in the 30-minute meetings. Make a note of your boss' expectations for the first 60 working days.

4. Meet a minimum of two external customers or clients and two of the most important internal customers excluding your boss. Complete notes on each of the meetings, which need to include the following details:

a. the quantum of the work that your team provides

b. RAG status of recent work and that of the last twelve months

c. the top three expectations from your team in the future

d. commentary on how well the governance process is working (frequency of meetings, escalation process, ease of doing business, etc.)

5. Meet the whole team, including the direct reporting managers who were previously met. This may require more than one meeting, depending on the size of the team and the geographical area across which it is spread. Cover the following:

a. Introduce yourself with a short biography, including career to date and free-time interests. This needs to be face to face. Avoid sending out an email introducing yourself; your boss should have done that. Demonstrate that you are approachable, have a sense of humour, and believe in empowering people as a means of delivering differentiated customer value.

b. Share a summary of what you have learnt from your meetings with your boss, direct reports (no mention of individuals), and customers. Ensure that you mention and acknowledge the past successes of the team. Recognising the team's past achievements will demonstrate that you have listened and learnt about the team that you are inheriting.

c. Provide the team with a one-page statement on expectations. This should cover what the team can expect from you and what you expect in return. This may include the following:

What you can expect from me:

- openness and honesty
- fairness and consistency in dealings with everyone
- empowerment to solve your own problems
- support when you need help
- approachable, 'always available, rarely required' (I saw this slogan printed on the side of a service van, and I have ever since adopted it as my style of approachable management.)
- recognition that we do not live in a perfect world and no one deliberately causes problems
- we all have bad days, but not bad months!

What I expect in return:

- a positive attitude: 'I can if...not I can't because' (see page 50–52 for further detail)
- no guessing; 'I don't know but will find out' is acceptable if not overused (see page 12)
- no surprises, escalate at the earliest warning sign, not the latest
- phone calls to you rather than emails (as this requires more thought and preparation. You can then ask for a summary email if required on what has been agreed)
- respect and trust for colleagues (see page 13)

- a commitment to achieve or exceed agreed objectives

Display the finally agreed list (one page maximum) in your office or your workstation prominently. Thus, everyone, including yourself, will be reminded of the foundational framework of mutual expectations. On day 20, you will have laid the foundation for your PSP.

Understand and implement (days 21 to 40)

During this period, you will need to acquire an all-round (360°) understanding of your team, your business unit and the relationships that are key to the ongoing success. You will establish a dialogue with your team, and they will come to know the environment that you wish to create for delivering differentiated customer value. You will also begin implementing the framework for success that you committed to execute to your boss. Your PSP will have its first 'valuation' from all the people you have met.

Actions for days 21 to 40

1. Set up a weekly call for your team. The call will be for team members to update their colleagues (and you) on the previous weeks' actions and achievements and those for the next two weeks. The attendance should be on a voluntary basis. In other words, people attend if they wish to. You should chair the call in the beginning and it should last no more than one hour. You will need to control the time to honour the one-hour commitment. Only overrun the meeting time in

extreme circumstances and with prior warning. You will know how many are on the call as they announce themselves, and you will need to manage their update time so that all the attendees can speak. Once the team is comfortable with the arrangement, you can invite other people who have a vested interest in your team's success to listen. Any follow-up actions can be taken offline after the call. I set this up as The Monday Call at 9 am every week (see page 41).

2. Become familiar with the key corporate processes and reporting timelines of your business unit. Quarterly updates, annual planning cycles, and employee appraisal cycles are some of these. Plot these on a calendar. Note and adhere to the lead times for submissions. Commit to being compliant with all corporate reporting requirements. Corporate compliance is table stakes for a meaningful personal share price.

3. Continue to meet with customers, suppliers, partner organisations, and individual team members. Make great efforts to remember the names of people, especially those of your own team. Keep a note of something interesting and personal about each team member from outside work. I have worked with a team member who was a fanatical supporter of the Barcelona football club. I also worked with a team member who was a qualified international cricket umpire, one who was a volunteer for the annual Glastonbury music festival, one who was an Olympic swimmer, and one who was in a rock

band, among many other interesting team members. Your PSP with your team will be greatly influenced by how you recognise and show interest in them. In this social media world, such knowledge is a pre-requisite.

4. Sometime between day 35 and 40, convene a half-day, all-hands meeting. At this meeting, you will conduct a flip chart session to answer the question, 'What is preventing us from being more successful?' You will need to run this session. The process and insights have been covered in detail in pages 43–45. From this session, you will know all the things that have been worrying the team and have been categorised into things that they can control, things they can influence, and things that are neither under their control nor influence. You will also have a list of things that can be done to develop the team and team members. This is a result of the second flip chart question: 'What is preventing me (individual team members) from being more successful?' From this activity, you will have understood a great deal about your team and what improvements are required. I cannot overemphasise the importance of this activity.

MADness (days 41 to 60)

This is the period when you and your team begin to Make-A-Difference (MADness). By now, you will have understood the things that are preventing even greater success for your team from the flip chart session in day 35–40. Regardless of how successful your team has been in the past, there is always room for improvement. As they begin to fix issues that are under their control, you have begun your liberation.

Actions for days 41 to 60

1. Send out a document to each team member on the outcome of the flip chart sessions conducted in the previous week. Only include the items that the team agreed were under their control or influence.

2. Conduct a 2–3 hour meeting with your direct reports on the actions that can be taken to improve the issues raised in the flip chart session. Make sure that they are time-bound and assigned to an individual. Minimise your own actions to emphasise the empowerment environment that you wish to create.

3. Share the results and actions from the flip chart session with your boss. Seek their support for actions where necessary. Once agreed, send out the list of actions and owners to the entire team. Thus, they will know that you, your boss, and your direct reports are committed to sustained improvement.

4. Continue with 'the Monday calls', but ask one or two direct reports to chair a call and manage the time. You, of course, will still listen in. Note any individuals who have failed to make the calls regularly and privately ask them the reason for their absence, bearing in mind that attendance is voluntary. Encourage them to participate in the

future, as the call is primarily for their benefit, not yours.

5. By this time, you will know who your best performers are. Tell them that you value their contribution and future support. This acknowledgement will be appreciated.

6. Find two things to stop doing. Popular examples are lengthy meetings and unnecessary administration tasks.

7. Develop a survey that can be used to monitor your PSP. This can be given to colleagues, customers (internal and external), and partners. It should include a measure of satisfaction in the early days of working with you. The questions might include: How easy am I to work with? How approachable am I? How easy is it to reach me when you need to? How well do I listen to you? How up to date do you think I am I with the issues facing us? How do you rate my fairness in dealing with people? How consistent am I in my dealings with people? What could I do to provide more value? This can be used, say, every six months and modified over time.

8. Congratulate yourself!

By day 60, you have:

- established your leadership style and framework
- come to know and worked with your direct reports and begun their empowerment, e.g. chairing the Monday call
- set expectations in both directions

- met customers, suppliers, partners, and other stakeholders' material for your future success
- committed to the compliance of your team to corporate reporting requirements and planning cycles
- come to know your team on a personal basis
- published a list of actions for improvement
- established a rapport with your boss, peers, and wider colleagues
- listened, learnt, understood, and implemented a considerable amount in order to be ready for the MADness and liberation to come

A word of caution

Not only do the so-called 30-60-90 day plans ignore the limits of the working week, they also ignore national holidays and assume no interruptions. It is highly likely that there will be activities that impact your team in the course of day-to-day business. Urgent actions may be required to deal with escalations. Corporate requests or your boss may require you to attend meetings at short notice. Activities in other parts of the business may divert resources that you were expecting, and so on. Thus, in my experience, I recommend using the 41–60 day period to complete any actions that may have been deferred from in the first 40 working days. When complete, however, do not forget to congratulate yourself on a job well done. Your personal IPO (Initial Public Offering) has been launched on the market, and your PSP will be higher than the expected contribution before you joined.

Liberation from coming second too often in sales

This chapter is especially for those people working in sales management. The previous chapters were more generic to the role of management. In sales management, the measure of success is very clear and binary; you either win a bid or lose it. This has a direct and tangible impact on performance. However, presence and behaviour will also play a significant role in improving win–loss ratios by providing a solid platform from which to gain support throughout the organisation, including board members. As will be explained from my personal experiences in this chapter, there are many moving parts in winning important contracts, which I call 'must-win' bids. A premium value PSP will undoubtedly ensure that crucial stakeholders from all parts of the business come together under your guidance. When funding is required, resources need to be reassigned, or innovative ideas need support, it is the PSP that will distinguish managers and their ability to gather the components required to win competitive deals. What follows is a series of ideas that I have implemented, which have resulted in superior performance. The ideas are grouped under the headings of Differentiation, Innovation, and Disruption, which together led to differentiated and superior performance over many years.

Optimising the win–loss ratio

I have spent most of my career associated with business units delivering IT services to corporate clients where deal cycles can be of several months. These deals generally follow a similar pattern. A prospective customer will identify a business need that requires the provision of IT services from third party suppliers to augment internal capability by upgrading or replacing existing systems. Typically, a prospective client will send out an invitation to tender (ITT) to a selected list of suppliers. A consulting firm may have advised the supplier list, and either that firm or the customer will publish a timetable of activities. This normally includes a pre-tender presentation by the customer, explaining their needs and priorities, followed by proposal submissions by suppliers and supplier presentations. From these activities, a shortlist will be drawn up for more detailed discussions with a down-selected two or three suppliers. During the shortlisting phase, the prospective customer will conduct supplier visits and request discussions with reference customers previously detailed in the proposal. Finally, a Best and Final Offer (BAFO) will be requested before the selection of the eventual winner for contract negotiations. A second supplier is normally held in reserve in case the contract negotiations flounder. However, in 95% of the cases, the original winner closes a mutually satisfactory contract.

The process is not exclusive to IT services, and many other industries recognise a similarly choreographed process. Such deal cycles for multi-million dollar contracts are costly in terms of time, money, and effort, and require the organisation's support. To ensure the commitment of the supplier organisation's resources, a bid qualification process is normally followed to garner senior executive support and the budget for submitting the bid. Deal bid budgets can often exceed $500K. As a consequence, qualifying the deal to ensure that the client's needs are in the sweet spot of supplier capability and experience is important. Once a 'go' decision has been agreed upon, the supplier then marshals the necessary resources to submit a winning bid.

The trouble is that a lost bid is a heavy burden on the bid lead, their team, and the supplier company. Most companies, therefore, keep track of their new business (gaining a new customer) bid–win ratio. In my experience, I have managed business units where the new business win proportion has moved from 1 in 10 to better than 1 in 3. This significant improvement was not just a consequence of better deal qualification (qualifying out of bidding where the customer needs were previously at the fringe of capability and experience) but rather of focusing on how to be different. Moving the bid-win ratio certainly improved my PSP and many of the initiatives mentioned below were copied by others. In a sales role winning bids against strong or incumbent competition is the rocket fuel of PSP.

In any competitive market, the surprising thing is how similar companies' offerings are, and not how different they are. I recall being part of the world's third-largest merger at the time when Burroughs bought Sperry to create Unisys. Once the merger was complete, each side presented its offerings to the other management team. It was frightening how similar the strengths of each company were. I then realised that customers must be seeing this similarity on a day-to-day basis. Bearing in mind that invitations to tender (ITTs) are subject to supplier pre-selection, the chance of similarity is even higher. Thus, it should be assumed that all supplier bids 'can do the job', and are similar in construct, and may only differ slightly. The bid commercials are where the difference most likely manifest, and depend on things like, the appetite to be competitive, the cost elements of the solution being proposed, the desired profit margin, and risk and contingency cost loadings. It is not, therefore, uncommon for losing bidders to claim that they 'lost on price'. However, in my experience, this is at best an excuse and at worst an inability or lack of understanding on 'how to price'.

When I was at Unisys, I inherited a business unit that sold IT solutions to the UK government and local government, called Public Services. The process for government procurement was prescriptive and strict in order to create a level playing field for bidders. Furthermore, to protect taxpayer investment, the process was not open to 'wining and dining', hospitality events, or inducements of any kind. Each ITT was published and publicly available in what was then called the European Journal and now the Official Journal of the European Union (OJEC). This was accessible to all potential bidders across Europe. Under the rules, there was no pre-selection of suppliers. Any company could bid. The prescriptive process included a weighted scoring matrix that included customer experience and compliance with requirements at each stage of the declared process. The intention was to ensure that the suppliers could provide the appropriate service at the lowest cost to the taxpayer. In summary, the lowest cost-compliant bid would win. The process followed the shortlisting of suppliers at an early stage to protect the government bid evaluation team from too much work, as many tens of bids could have been submitted. The bid evaluation process was also transparent such that if a bid was lost, the bidder was entitled to a debrief on why they had lost and what their weighted scores had been relative to the winning bid.

I describe this because it is an example of the levelest playing field that I have come across for bidders. Also, the government procurement process meant that the bids were subject to internal audit and, in the event of a supplier challenge to the final decision, public scrutiny. In short, then, the process was designed to ensure that the winning bid was indeed the best value for money for the taxpayer.

In the first several months of my tenure of the Public Services business unit, we bid and lost four deals. At each debrief with the customer, we learnt that pricing and overall solution design did not represent the best value. Each time, we applied the learning from the customer debrief and looked forward to the next bid, despite the frustration that was growing in the team by the time of the fourth bid.

For the fifth bid, we decided only to submit a proposal if the requirement was a no-brainer for qualification. In other words, the selected bid would have to play to our core strengths and capabilities backed by excellent customer references and compelling commercials. This would be our best chance of winning. A few weeks later, such a bid profile emerged, and it scored the highest marks in our internal bid qualification process. We solicited board approval and duly agreed to bid. To ensure that we had the best chance of winning, we assembled the 'best and brightest' team from sales, solutioning, and delivery. These highly skilled people were reassigned to the bid where necessary. By the time of the submission, we had the best team, a world-beating solution, and the important chemistry connection with the client decision makers and influencers. As we went through the various stages of the bid cycle, the feedback was positive. Our bid was shortlisted, and after successful customer reference visits, we eventually submitted our BAFO and awaited the announcement. It was not long in coming. We had lost again! With all the previous learning applied, best of the best resources, and a compelling solution and commercials, we were crestfallen and deeply depressed. What to do? A debrief was requested, and this time I invited our CFO and Chief Marketing Officer to attend rather than the bid team.

The debrief was very revealing. The customer began by saying that the team had done a great job and that they really enjoyed working with the bid lead, who was one of my team members. We learnt that the scoring evaluation was done under 13 different headings. On 6 of the scores, our bid was within 5% of the winning bid. From previous loss reviews, we knew that the winning score must not be greater than 5% than the runner up. Of the remaining seven scores, we were astonished to hear that in 4 of the 7, our bid was up to 80% more expensive than the winning bid. We could not believe it. After understanding a few more points that were not material, we went back to our office and relooked at our bid. The margins were low single digits on the 4 identified outliers. This for a seven-year deal. How could anyone be so much cheaper than us? We were determined to dig deeper, and a lengthy analysis took place that proved to be very enlightening. On the hardware bid, which was 60% of the proposal components, we had included newly released computers. The assumption was that new is better. We discovered that in pricing all the new hardware releases, our head office included a cost for populating the geographies with spare parts. Understandable, but unhelpful in this case! Thus, any new hardware included an additional cost for spare parts. Secondly, we noticed that we had proposed 35% more disk storage than was specified in the ITT. This was because the disk unit alternatives were just under the ITT specification. We thought more was good! Worst still, we thought that the extra would be valued.

The thorough analysis also revealed that we had proposed using sub-contractors for part of the work that needed our margin added to their cost and margin. We eventually came to understand why we were so far in excess of the winning bid on the 4 items. This led me to the conclusion that we needed to better understand 'the rules of pricing to win'.

1. Understand how unit pricing is derived from factory to customer for all components. Understand how the component prices are constructed. Request exceptions for large 'must-win' bids with regard to things like spare parts cost loading.

2. The government, and perhaps others, will not pay for 'gold plating'. So, price for the disk space they need, even if it comes with more, anything else can be a later possibly priced upgrade. This will usually require finance exception approval.

3. There is no additional value in new hardware units. Typically, when new hardware is released, the older models are discounted. Propose the older, perfectly adequate models with plenty of spare parts!

4. Think carefully before using sub-contractors and the additional margin that you need to make on their margin. Negotiate with sub-contractors, and

be transparent about what is needed. They only win if you win!

5. Socialise all of the above and other learnings with the senior management.

6. Only apply the learning for bids that you have agreed are 'must win'. Otherwise, you dilute the margin across the board.

7. However, the most valuable learning element that was changed in subsequent bids was introducing the concept of 'The Get Well Plan'. If you need a low margin to win government bids, what is the plan to improve the margin during the lifetime of the contract? Typically 5 to 7 years. This period is long enough to have an acceptable lifetime deal margin and will inevitably require upgrades during the life of the contract.

The Get Well Plan

The fifth bid described included an item for future upgrade costs for various elements of the ITT. We discovered at debriefing that this did not form a part of the 13 scored items in the evaluation. Thus, future upgrades could be charged at a higher rate or even list price. Furthermore, the contract was for seven years. Thus, the winning bid would have six years to recover from a low margin in the first year. We eventually developed this into a well-crafted programme that I called 'The Get Well Plan'. This allows a low bid at proposal time and results in losing bidders claiming 'they bought the business', when in fact there was a holistic, or lifetime, view taken of this 'must-win' deal that was supported by the board.

Following this ultimate and painful deal lesson, we subsequently bid for 12 large contracts in the following eighteen months and won 9 of them! A win ratio of 75%! This was not my reckoning but proffered by the head of the government IT procurement at a review meeting with our board. He disclosed that we had become the most successful bidder of IT services to the government over the previous eighteen months. So, the homework and pain eventually paid off. The summary is as follows:

1. Understand the rules of winning and pricing to win.
2. Ensure that you know how the components of costs are made up.
3. Seek guidance on substituting compliant components that carry less cost.
4. Develop a Get Well Plan, from the outset to be disclosed internally, on how to recover margin over time.

The learning from this experience has proved valuable in non-government bids, as the concepts are equally applicable in highly competitive markets. Needless to say, for 'must-win' deals, the Get Well Plan has been implemented in all the business units that I have worked in since. And the margin recovery has indeed been achieved over the life of the contracts.

In the private sector, there are more dynamics at play and merely being the lowest cost-compliant bid is not enough to win. A bid that is very similar to competitors bids, we called a 'me too' bid. This can prevail in government procurement. Indeed, it could be argued that it is the goal: a 'me too' bid at no more than 5% higher cost than the second-placed bidder. But in the wider commercial world, 'me too' is simply not good enough.

From 'me too' to D.I.D.

A 'me too' bid (very similar others) will never win with a new customer in the commercial world. A 'me too' bid may win with an existing customer but will warn the customer about other bidders closing in on your territory. Thus, it is the safest to assume that a 'me too' bid will never win in a new client situation. I believe this because, in my experience, there are always extraneous factors at play, particularly outside the public sector bids.

All bids include multiple components and moving parts. These naturally include decision makers, recommenders, and influencers on the customer side. Each of these individuals has a network of colleagues, past and present, who may play a part in the bid process. In the background, consulting firms advise the board, not necessarily concerning the bid per se, but eventually, their opinion is sought in the general discussion, if not formally. Also, assume that the 'golf club' syndrome is at work. Influencers, recommenders, and decision makers invariably discuss their business matters with their social colleagues, and they have an opinion based on recent or past experience, rumour, or hearsay. The media may also play a part in articles or programmes exposing companies' successes, difficulties, practices, or scams and scandals. Being referenced in that mix may or may not help. Industry analysts publish their supplier evaluations, Gartner's Magic Quadrants and the like, which are used to flatter or scupper a bidder's credentials. Thus, it is safe to assume that there will be 100-plus interactions (I exaggerate for effect) outside any formal bid process, each of which can trip you up or enhance your bid. The point is, you are never likely to know. So, the odds of winning by a nose with a 'me too' bid is negligible. So, what is to be done?

A few years ago, when I was at HCL, we came close to losing one of our largest accounts, putting at risk a $50 million annual revenue. The account was then one of the top-20 global accounts for HCL. The possible loss was nothing to do with services delivery, which was excellent. In fact, we became a potential victim of industry consolidation in our customers' market. There were two competing companies in the same market, our client had not performed well over a period, and was rumoured to be taken over. Sure enough, a competing company eventually agreed to a takeover of our client. Both companies had large businesses and employed well over 10,000 people in each entity. Between the two companies, there were four preferred suppliers of similar IT services. One of the suppliers was present in both companies, but our company was only present in the acquired entity. So, the supplier landscape for services was as follows:

Company 1   Company 2 (acquired)

    X.................common to both.................... X
    Y...HCL
    Z

Some years earlier, Company 1 had come out to tender for outsourced IT services, and for whatever reasons, HCL was not invited to tender.

In these circumstances, it is inevitable that the acquiring company dominates the agenda for establishing a newly formed company, which includes IT services. The preferred platforms would be expected to be from Company 1, and there would be a migration of systems from Company 2 to Company 1.

As a part of the integration programme, Company 1 IT management stated that they wanted a group of no more than three suppliers for similar IT services. This would ensure healthy competition while being workable from a supplier management viewpoint. Things were not looking well for HCL. Company 1 already had three preferred suppliers, and supplier X was common to both the companies. The obvious question was, 'why do we need a fourth supplier?' Particularly since the acquiring company had no experience of HCL services. Clearly, at best, HCL could expect to be kept for a period of transition to a consolidated IT landscape. However, in the longer term, there was no obvious reason why a fourth supplier should exist. I then realised that we had to be seen as different, probably very different, in order to justify having a fourth preferred partner for albeit similar IT services.

We had over 800 people working on IT services for Company 2, and our delivery team had done a good job consistently. But so had X, Y, and Z, for company 1. Clearly, service quality was not a strong enough differentiator to justify a fourth preferred supplier. While the takeover was in progress, over three months, we had a number of internal meetings to decide our course of action. In terms of 'me too', we should have expected to exit the account. But that was a pill too bitter to swallow. We had to do something drastic and material. Eventually, after a series of planning sessions involving the delivery and account team, we emerged with the seeds of our success. Three simple words would describe our plan. We agreed that the only way we would deserve to become a valued partner of the new customer entity would be if we could demonstrate that we were:

- Differentiated
- Innovative
- and Disruptive

Thus, the acronym D.I.D. was created. In the beginning, not all of the teams were convinced that this was the answer or that it would work. Hence, some coaching and persuasion had to take place to convince a few team members that this was indeed our best chance of prevailing in the longer term. Once we had enough people onboard, the momentum picked up. The account and delivery teams were then tasked with developing the proof points for the three tenets – D.I.D. What evidence could we muster to prove differentiation, innovation and disruption? A procurement and IT visit was due to each of the 4 suppliers in two months, and by then, we had to have developed the evidence for D.I.D and present it in a compelling form.

By the time of the visit, we were in good shape. The teams had developed compelling evidence of where HCL was truly differentiated, innovative, and disruptive. Not only that, but the evidence and proof points could be equally beneficial to other clients. The ideas were repeatable. Below is an extract of some of the D.I.D elements that were relevant to our needs of the day. The point is not the relevance of the particular points but rather the need for every team to develop their own D.I.D plan to thrive in increasingly competitive markets. The list of D.I.D. initiatives below should, therefore, be an incentive to develop similar ideas relevant to your needs.

From the customer visit that was a make-or-break occasion for us, the D.I.D elements that the team created were as follows:

Differentiated

Here we had something of a head start because our company had adopted the *EFCS* programme. This has already been mentioned in earlier chapters. You will recall that it was developed from a realisation that employees who directly work with customers are where customer value is created – *The Value Zone.*

Lunch with the Transformers

When the customer visitors came during the takeover process, as part of the agenda, we asked the customer team to be hosted at lunch by the Value Creators who had worked on the Company 2 account for a few years. This group lunch did not include any managers or senior executives. At lunch, the customer team could ask any questions they liked from the Value Creators. It worked a treat. The customer team did not want to finish the session, and they were deeply impressed by the young people, their knowledge of their customer's business, their critique of what they (the customer) could do better, and the enthusiasm and quality of the team. Since it was so successful, this developed into a regular feature of all subsequent customer visits called 'Lunch with the Transformers'. Note that no managers being present was the key. This demonstrated that value was indeed created at the working level and not the management level. The strange thing for me is that these sessions are often the highlight of customer visits, and yet, by virtue of no manager or senior executive presence, I have not personally experienced what happens.

One customer revealed to me that after experiencing 'Lunch with the Transformers', he had asked other companies to arrange a similar event, but had been declined. This aroused his suspicions of the extent of senior management orchestration arranged by other companies.

No PowerPoint

It is not uncommon that customer visits to delivery centres in India or elsewhere are dominated by PowerPoint slides – 'Death by PowerPoint', as we called it. On the occasion of the Company 2 visit, I decided that the full-day agenda would have no PowerPoint slides. We began somewhat provocatively by saying 'we can show you PowerPoint in London, on this visit, we want you to meet the people who deliver service value to you.' The main boardroom had a flip chart on which presenters of various topics could write to explain a point further; but mostly, the day was dominated by short introductory comments on previously agreed agenda items followed by a lengthy Q&A session and discussion. Ours was the only company visit that was not PowerPoint heavy. Again, 'No PPT' became a regular feature of subsequent customer visits. Conducting the day's agenda with no slides allowed a frank and open discussion on many points of interest. What was valued was the dialogue with the subject matter experts that could hold their own and constructively challenge the customer team. One prop that we used was visible in the main meeting room. We had put up on the wall square Post-it notes with the signature of everyone that had ever worked on the account. Thus, over 1000 post-it notes were covering the walls. This gave a powerful visual image of the amount of retained knowledge and experience in delivering quality work to Company 2 (the acquired company) over several years.

Customer Value Portal

This was a natural differentiator for HCL, as already mentioned. Over the three years before the takeover, the value creators who worked on the account had developed and submitted many ideas that had been accepted by Company 2. Each value-added idea was created from team members, suggesting additional or alternative ways to improve efficiency and effectiveness or reduce cost. The total of the value signed off by the customer had reached £2.41 M.

Thus, in the agenda session on *value-added services*, I presented the customer Chief Information Officer (CIO) from Company 1, with a spoof (4ft by 3ft) cheque with 'Two million four hundred and ten thousand pounds' written on it. The CIO and his team were delighted, and we had a picture taken of the presentation. The cheque still hangs in the local customer office. Again, no other supplier (X, Y, or Z) had ever produced anything similar in signed off value creation more than the contract. This again was a powerful visual aid to demonstrate that we were indeed differentiated.

Customer Experience Room

The fourth differentiator for the day was to have the customer team walk around a room with posters on the wall and a large table with PCs and mobile devices on it. The room had a sign on the door: 'Customer 1 Experience Room'. The posters followed the theme of how our company could add value in future years to the newly created entity. This involved the most preparation prior to the visit. The delivery team had analysed the overall customer IT landscape covering both hardware and software. From this, they developed a 5-year plan on how the software and hardware landscape could transform. They also estimated the cost savings of the various initiatives by each year. The total over five years was a cost saving of £185 M – a considerable sum. But the cleverest part of what they had done was to match each initiative against the strategic objectives that the customer board had publicised (in the course of their own 5-year plan). Finally, the posters were arranged by year, by initiative, and by cost reduction for each strategic objective. This resulted in a 3-dimensional view of initiatives. Each poster was then spoken of by one of the team members and questions answered.

The customer team were most impressed and confirmed that they had not seen anything like it before. Cutting the transformation initiatives by each of the views allowed the customer to appreciate which initiatives could be prioritised. These would be those initiatives with the greatest saving, ease of implementation, and best fitting with the strategic objectives. During the discussion on various topics, the PCs and mobile devices were used to explain and demonstrate elements of the posters further. The session ended with a mini-workshop listing what actions the customer wanted our team to take when they returned to the UK. This was a true sign that we were making progress in becoming a long-term partner and justifying a fourth supplier of similar services but with a differentiated outlook.

The next objective was to evidence our ideas on innovation, our second tenet of D.I.D.

Innovative

At any time in the recent years, IT has gone through tremendous change and continues to be the preferred platform for initiatives like improved end-customer connection, faster product introduction, business analytics-driven insights, robotics, and cost reduction through automation. To demonstrate our generic capability, our company had previously set up two Innovation Laboratories – one in London and one in Singapore. For this particular visit, we created a mock Innovation Lab for this single customer. This involved demonstrating applications that the team had developed for mobile devices, video and self-service. The applications were stand alone but used the customer logo and brand colouring. The 'art of the possible' was then demonstrated. Again, this was shown as exhibits in a separate room with a sign on the door 'Customer 1 Innovation Lab'. We continued the day with no PowerPoint, so each mini demonstration was presented by a team member and resulting customer questions were answered. This format soon became a standard for other accounts.

Three demonstrations were done simultaneously with the customer team split into three groups of four. When each demonstration was complete, the customer groups moved around. In all, there were 6 demonstrations. To maximise the number of demonstrations in the time allocated, the six demo stations were numbered and rotated as 1, 3, and 5, followed by 2, 4, and 6. This removed the chance of too much simultaneous talking spoiling the showcase.

Proposal on a page

Occasionally, an Invitation to Tender (ITT) from a customer will stipulate a limit on the number of pages that a response can have. More commonly, there is no such requested limit. Thus, proposals can either be too short covering only the essential details or too long so as to lose your way in the reading. For this particular customer visit, we had been asked to propose how we might work with the customer as a preferred supplier after the takeover. Naturally, there was an enormous amount of work that we had delivered prior to the takeover of Company 2 with some 800 staff deployed over five years. This background provided much evidence and proof of a track record of on-time and to-budget service delivery. Also, for project delivery excellence, the account team had developed preferred 'ways of working' with the customer. This included forms for ideas for future technology development, commercial arrangements, critical success factors, and importantly, HR considerations on how to get the best out of the partnership.

In order to bring all the components to answer the exam question into a compelling and innovative format, we invented 'Proposal-on-a-Page'. The page concerned was an A0 size (approx. 3' x 4'), where each of the aspects of our proposal was pictorially represented.

- **Section 1** – a summary of the customers' objectives as expressed by themselves
- **Section 2** – design overview on working together
- **Section 3** – the technology map on which system transformation could evolve
- **Section 4** - the proposed programme management methodology
- **Section 5** – over time what quantified benefits would manifest
- **Section 6** – a list critical success factors for the programme, do's and dont's
- **Section 7** – common pitfalls (things to avoid from other experiences)
- **Section 8** – the HR summary of skills, training, and suggested ways of working
- **Section 9** – the proposed governance structure
- **Section 10** – showing how using sections 2 to 9 can be used to meet the objectives in Section 1

The Proposal-on-a-Page not only proved beneficial in the articulation of the 360-degree nature for mutual value, but also fully articulated the proposal solution. In fact, the customer lead asked to take a copy of the A0 sheet away, to be used as an example of a 360-degree view of working together.

This became a compelling one pager and was adopted for many other proposals for many other customers. The Proposal-on-a-Page became a standard tool to bring clarity and completeness to many a situation. The artefact has been repeatedly acknowledged as innovative and a great prop for boardroom presentations. The layout can be customised, and extracts from a proposal can be incorporated. However, this should not just be a cut and paste of slides. The page must look like the singular prepared item representing all the elements of a proposal such that while standing with the page mounted on a wall, all elements of the proposal can be explained while keeping the bigger picture in view.

Betting game

The betting game is very useful in checking that priorities for objectives are agreed upon and that the actions to achieve the most important objectives have executive alignment. The betting game provides a means of exploring priorities and revealing any issues with executive team alignment. There is sometimes an issue with what customers see as important and the alignment of the customer's senior management, let alone other workers, on priorities. It can be difficult, therefore, for a potential supplier of services to understand what to focus on. Speaking to different stakeholders can reveal different priorities, and at worst, divergence from the agreed board and published objectives. The challenge for a supplier is how to respond to a situation where customer executives are not agreed or aligned to an objective or means of achieving it. One innovation that worked for me was the introduction of a betting game when such situations arose. This not only brings out the issues of difference or customer alignment but does it in a non-confrontational way that is in fact fun. It also positions the services company as a most professional partner.

Take the case where a customer had adopted and socialised a set of preferred behaviours for their business. These were written up on worksite posters and published on the intranet. The preferred behaviours would be recognisable to most companies – things like 'we are open and honest', 'we support our colleagues', 'we achieve our objectives as a team', 'we do not talk behind people's backs', etc. The frequent challenge is the alignment to the behaviours and what actions are taken to support them.

In a particular case, I recall that a CIO of a large company had come up with some measures to promote the desired behaviours similar to those mentioned above. These included the following:

- To promote openness and honesty, the CIO introduced a weekly phone-in for his entire team (some 400 colleagues) for a no-holds-barred Q&A.
- To promote transparency, he produced a monthly published account of progress against key objectives that was sent to all 400 colleagues.

- To promote supporting colleagues and working as a team, he introduced a six monthly employee satisfaction survey.
- There were several other initiatives that the CIO took to help promote the desired behaviours so that his team would respond to change faster and become a better service provider to their internal business colleagues.

However, after over a year of such actions as he put it, 'the needle had not moved'; for example, the employee satisfaction had similar scores. Needless to say, the CIO was not sure why all the effort had not paid greater dividends. There was due to be an all-hands meeting with his team in a month's time, and he asked what experience from our *Employee First* programme might prove helpful. He had read the book, and in fact, ordered copies for each of his 400 staff members.

There were clearly some issues associated with buy-in from his team regarding the desired behaviours and alignment with them. Maybe some members of the senior team were not walking the talk, perhaps lip service was prevalent, or the members of the senior team were not aligned and offering different perspectives to their teams.

What had proved effective with other customers when addressing similar challenges was to play the 'betting game'. This would tangibly and openly test the team alignment, priorities, and actions required to bring the strategy to life. This is very effective as it involves people openly discussing important principles but with the added fun of using betting chips to express their individual priorities. A summary of the game is as follows:

To begin the game, a clear statement needs to be agreed upon. A real-life example was working with a retailer that wanted to create a sense of 'inspiring ownership' in its managers and workforce. The idea was that by inspiring individual ownership, business performance would improve, and collaboration would increase as each employee would be behaving as an 'owner' of the business. The company executive organised a number of workshops for groups of 20 managers each to socialise the desired behaviours. The betting game was included on the agenda, and I was invited to facilitate the sessions so as to provide feedback on what each group of 20 managers thought the most appropriate traits were to achieve the desired behaviours. At the appropriate time, the delegates were each given chips with which to 'bet' on their preferred priorities.

The statement that the executives agreed on which bets would be placed was as follows:

'The most important traits for employees to demonstrate inspiring ownership are:'

Ten traits were identified, against which groups of employees could prioritise and weigh their preferences for achieving the objective of inspiring ownership. These were the following:

1. Work tirelessly to build greater engagement.
2. Create a climate for personal responsibility.
3. Inform and gain commitment to change.

4. Create and generate ownership for ideas and solutions.
5. Share knowledge as the key to empowerment.
6. Clear issues to shift from paternalistic to empowerment.
7. Inspire others to take responsibility.
8. Involve the team soonest for change and initiatives.
9. Hold honest conversations about challenges and threats.
10. Create opportunities for employees to develop solutions.

Ten A4-sized sheets were put on a table, each with the main question at the top and one of the ten traits written underneath. The ten sheets of paper were spread out on a large table, away from where the delegates were sitting. The ten sheets were spread out so that when the bets (chips) were placed, there was no chance of the chips overlapping another trait.

Each workshop participant was given ten chips, from which they could place 'bets' on a maximum of three of the ten traits. The delegates weighting of the bet would be expressed by the split of the ten chips. All ten chips on one trait made it pre-eminent; a more balanced bet across a maximum of three traits would result in a 3,3,4 spread. However, a maximum of three bets only could be placed using all ten chips for each participant.

The question and ten traits were put up on a screen and discussed briefly to ensure that the participants were clear on how to play the game. The participants were then asked to privately write down the bets on a piece of paper that only they could see. They would write down up to three traits and their split of ten chips. This was done so that when the participants were asked to physically place their chips on the table with the ten sheets of paper on it, they would not be persuaded to change by seeing where the other bets went. In other words, they would remain true to their original private viewpoint.

Once each participant had placed their bets, a clear and visible pattern would emerge on the collective view of traits most likely to achieve the objective of 'inspiring ownership'. The bets could then be counted, and a list of traits of the most popular to the least popular identified and discussed.

At this point, there was a view of collective priorities. For the three most popular statements (most chips), a second betting game was done. This involved the team agreeing to nine actions that could be taken to deliver each of the three most popular traits from the first betting round. This time, a ten-chip spread bet (maximum three bets with ten chips) across the nine actions that needed to be taken to ensure the most important traits, identified by the first bet, was to be achieved. This second bet involved creating nine more A4 sheets, this time with the wording at the top of each of the nine actions being 'the actions we need to take to implement trait (1, 2, 3 in order) are:' followed by each of the nine different actions. By the end of the session and across all sessions, the senior executive had real evidence of the management's collective view on what needed to be done to 'inspire ownership' in their business. Furthermore, it was a collective management view, and not a top-down diktat. This in itself inspired ownership.

This process is highly interactive and fun to do and participate in. Furthermore, it provides real-time information on group thinking that can be repeated across workshops with different participants, to provide an evidence-based, consolidated view. The published results are far more likely to be adhered to and owned, as each participant is involved and allowed to express their personal view.

I have run such sessions with groups of as few as eight board members to entire department teams of 400 participants in one session. The larger session was ,in fact, the one with the CIO I referred to at the beginning of this section. Due to the number of participants, the betting papers were put on a stage with a camera above the stage, revealing the emerging result as groups of 40 colleagues bet at a time. The betting papers were each 3 metres by 3 metres, not A4! In the end, there were 4000 chips on the stage and a clear pattern of top 3 selections. When all the bets were later counted and published a few days later, the CIO changed the priority of actions he had previously thought important. Indeed, one of his top three priorities before the session turned out to be in the bottom two when voted on by his 400 staff.

The betting game has proved to be a real innovation to customers and, in my experience, is much valued as a means of bringing clarity and collective views to the fore. I suggest practising the betting game internally to become familiar and confident with its working before conducting a session with customers.

Tomorrow's news today

Frequently, when a proposal is made, it is made on the assumption that it is for achieving some future objective for the customer. The proposal, therefore, includes an implementation plan, pricing, and timescale for achieving the desired outcome. For example, a given high street bank may want to be the best at customer service within three years. Let us assume it is independently rated as being the fourth best currently. Becoming recognised as the best for customer service needs some external validation from an independent source, like a market research company, to be credible. With the growth in self-service technology and mobile devices, an improvement in customer service will likely require investment in IT services, marketing, and training for customer contact points including tellers, brokers, and call centres. To realise it, in fact, a high street bank in the UK did actually mail its customers in 2016 with a booklet entitled *Becoming The Best Bank For Customers*. The booklet reiterated the goal and detailed the progress made on the main objectives. The bank set many measurable objectives on the journey in order to achieve the declared goal.

Returning to a non-specific example to monitor the progress towards the goal of becoming the best for customer service, various milestones need to be identified, which might include the following:

- Lowest number of customer complaints within two years
- Highest percentage of self-service customers within three years

- Highest percentage of online users in 18 months
- Largest number of mobile application users in a year
- Fastest settlement for payments in 18 months
- Single-customer view for all customer products and services within two years

When the objective and the actions are known and achieved, the future state can be assumed.

One way of demonstrating that the customer service journey is well understood is to write a news article from a date in the future. This can make the objective come alive and be a fun way of confirming that you recognise what business benefit your proposal is intended to achieve. This is important, because too often the business objectives of a proposal are lost in the technology gobble-de-gook.

The fun part is making the article look authentic. For a case in point, an article can be created for an imaginary newspaper with a logo, date and column layout. An eye-catching headline should be added to lead the article. The journal date needs to be a date that is three to five years hence. Thus, in the example suggested above, the result might be as follows:

The Centurion Times – date 8-2-2022
New York
Finance Section
Headline: XYZ Bank is voted best for customers

Article:

Just three years ago, XYZ Bank had more customer complaints than its three closest rivals. Customers had to wait longer for payments, and the bank had been fined over $500K for breaching client money regulations. Now, just three years later, it is the darling of consumer groups and is topping the polls. They have attracted more customers in the last three years than the previous ten. This extraordinary turnaround has been achieved by a series of investments that began in 2017 under the banner 'putting customers first'. Nearly 2 million customers switched their current and savings accounts to XYZ in the last twelve months. In a consumer survey, Which? magazine asked more than 10,500 people how happy they were with their bank's responsiveness, value for money, and dependability. It used the results to calculate an overall score on customer satisfaction and how likely they were to recommend their bank to a friend. XYZ bank achieved an overall score of 76%, compared to an average of 58% for the sector.

The CEO of XYZ Bank, Mr Norman Smith, was on a panel championing customer service at the World Economic Forum in Davos yesterday. He said 'in achieving our aim of being best for customer service in our chosen market, I pay tribute to the technology investments we have made, supported by a team of believers who made it happen.' In his Davos presentation,

Mr Smith showed how customer self-service and mobile banking had exceeded their expectations, resulting in a Best Bank award for customers from the Retail Banking Association. He also said that the customers now have a single statement where they can see all their holdings, from cash to mortgage, savings, investments and insurances, in one place. Mr Smith claims that no other bank can currently do this.

End of article

An article like this is not difficult or time consuming to construct. It is not only a point of interest and innovation for customers but also a useful aid to the employees creating a tender response, and it should form a part of the executive summary as an insert.

The above are some of the ideas created to demonstrate innovation in an otherwise 'me too' market.

The final part of D.I.D. is Disruptive.

Disruptive

Disruption is a peculiar word, as a disruption in one's life is generally a negative thing. However, I contend that while disruptive children are a bad thing, disruptive business partners should be welcomed. In the case of the bank takeover mentioned earlier, having a fourth preferred supplier who is no different from the rest would not have added anything to the customer except increasing supplier management cost and effort. However, a disruptive supplier in that mix may well be welcome to stir things up and keep everyone on their toes.

I contend that the time spent on how your company can be a disruptive business partner will pay handsome dividends. In my dealings with customers, I like to bring out the fact that they should consider a disruptive partner as a welcome ally, especially in a mix of other preferred suppliers. The ideas that have worked for me include the following:

Same for less

Commit to doing the same work next year for less money than this year. In fact, I recommend that you guarantee it! This is a powerful proposition, as, in a services industry, the costs generally increase year-on-year as employment cost and inflation increase. However, by guaranteeing the same for less, you are duty bound to focus on future efficiencies to avoid margin reduction. For example, increasing the element of automation in a system or improving the incidents of one-and-done actions to reduce rework and testing costs. Also consider process improvements and cycle time reduction. This is disruptive in nature, as other suppliers will not welcome the initiative as they seek to increase their share of wallet. Interestingly, when 'the same for less' was implemented across selected accounts, we found it possible to reduce the cost to the customer and improve our margin. This is because more automation means fewer people, and process improvement reduces cycle times and effort. The focus on cycle time reduction proved valuable in delivering quantifiable customer value. This initiative meant that any customer process that could be measured in cycle time could be reduced.

- procure to pay (cycle time)
- mean time to repair faults (cycle time)
- response to customer queries (cycle time)
- regulatory reporting (cycle time)
- annual report publication (cycle time), and so on...

The next idea we implemented as a disruptive business partner was that of cannibalising revenue.

Cannibalising revenue

This philosophy, when successful, will reduce your revenue! The idea of cannibalisation is that you spend time looking to see which revenue streams can be reduced or ended. Why on earth would you do this? There are two supporting thoughts. The first is that, by definition, your company is one of the few preferred suppliers for similar services. All suppliers look to increase their revenue, not decrease it. But sooner or later, there is a cost reduction initiative or a vendor consolidation exercise that puts your revenue at risk. Too often, suppliers are caught out when this happens and are in reactive mode from the outset – wrong footed, you might say. Alternatively, a technological advance might result in the automation or elimination of services. Examples would be the Internet of Things (IOT) and Robotics. These represent technological disruption, which is a well-established reality with driverless cars and process automation. The idea, therefore, is that if you do not seek to cannibalise your revenue, others will. It also demonstrates that you see customer value creation as a long-term proposition.

The second reason is that it just makes sense and can only be seen by customers as a positive contribution to your partnership. This has proved valuable to support the notion that service suppliers exist to deliver differentiated customer value.

The blind faith part is that you can look for, or be considered for, additional work in some other area. This is not guaranteed but is highly likely when you have demonstrated a willingness to cannibalise your own revenue stream. Thus, a pre-emptive proposal on cannibalising revenue can include suggestions on where the revenue reduction could be spent to add value overall. For example, most IT landscapes have legacy systems and duplicate or redundant code and applications. These come with a disproportionately high maintenance cost, as older technologies require specialist skills that are often priced at a premium. The cost of amending these systems is also high in testing before deployment.

In one company, our team agreed to take the risk of reducing the cost of maintenance, given a portfolio of applications to maintain while improving the support levels and reducing the level of historical incidents as a result of system failures. This was a compelling proposition, reducing cost and improving service and system availability. Following a short due diligence period, we quoted a fixed price for maintaining a suite of applications for the following three years. The fixed price was 30% lower than the existing maintenance cost for the customer. A compelling proposition that was accepted. The challenge for us was to develop ideas and plans to provide the improved service at the quoted price with a suitable margin. Over the next 12 months, seven initiatives were designed to deliver the results with an acceptable margin. It worked and led to more and more applications coming our way. Thus, we cannibalised our own revenue and our competitor's revenue, where they were previously maintaining the applications. This is a classic example of cannibalised revenue producing more overall revenue!

Reinvest 2% of revenue

This is the third disruptive proposition that, at first sight, also reduces revenue and profit. However, for larger engagements, it is an eye-catching proposal that customers will see value in. Future revenue streams from customers are usually unclear; thus, a commitment to reinvest some of the existing revenue will allow prototyping and proof of concepts (POC) to be developed to inform future investment opportunities. What is not in doubt is that technological innovation continues apace. Thus, there will always be new capabilities that need to be understood and decisions taken as to the efficacy and viability of a new technology.

When I ask CIOs about how much their IT budgets increase year-on-year above inflation, they look at me strangely and laugh. The fact is that year after year, the IT budget attracts an inflationary increase at best. Industry survey after survey indicates that only 10% of IT departments receive an above-inflation annual budget increase and that for over 60%, the budget is flat or reduced. I then ask what percentage of the IT budget is spent on 'run the business' (RTB, keeping the lights on) as opposed to 'change the business' (CTB). Typically, 60% to 80% of the budget is spent on RTB. It is likely, therefore, that a CIO has a flat budget from one year to the next and must spend the vast majority of the IT budget on maintaining the status quo. Within that, the CIO needs to accommodate wage inflation for his in-house team.

The next question that I ask CIOs concerns the board of directors.

I ask if the board appetite for technology-enabled change has increased, decreased, or stayed the same. In over 80% of cases, the response is that the board's appetite has increased dramatically, especially in recent years. There is a growing momentum associated with the Internet of Things (IOT), cyber and digital technologies, robotics, business analytics, artificial intelligence (AI), and customer experience management and the continuing rise of mobile applications and cloud-based services.

The final question that I ask is how much of the CTB budget is allocated to regulatory compliance. 'Around half' is the usual response. Of course, regulatory compliance is a must. It always trumps any other investment. Thus, CIOs can look forward to only around 10–20% of their total budget being allocated to business-related change. This is against a disproportionate increase in appetite from the board for technology-enabled transformation. Thus, the likelihood of CIOs using their precious budget for speculative investment to assess new technologies is very low.

Returning to the reinvestment of revenue, the logic is that the reinvestment of 2% of the supplier's annual revenue can be used to develop prototypes and POCs to provide demonstrable artefacts that can be shown to the board. For the POCs that achieve board priority, the business case can be developed and additional funds requested. This will help to sort the board priorities between the wishful and needful projects. The chances that these projects come to the partner that invested in developing the POC at their own cost will increase. There will also be direct prior-project experience, providing a head start over competitors. There are no guarantees, but at worst, there will be an advantage if competitive tendering is invoked.

All of the disruptive ideas mentioned above have been implemented in business units that I have run, and although there is no causal link, my business unit grew at twice the pace of the company overall over the most recent 5-year period. All disruption involves risk, so an early test of one's own company's appetite for risk is required.

In this section, I have tried to distinguish between a disruptive idea and a sensible commercial proposition. Writing a contract on a risk–reward basis, whereby the supplier and customer share in the benefits of a given commercial construct subject to some thresholds, is not considered as disruptive here. The benchmark that I prefer to use as a test of disruption is one that your competitors will not want to engage in and where they will have to expend much internal effort in getting approval to match your proposal. Thus, all disruption, by my definition, will carry first mover advantage and wrongfoot the competition.

The D.I.D results

It would be reasonable to ask what proof points there were from the initiatives above and where they were sustained. In the example mentioned of the Company 1 and Company 2 merger, HCL became a long-standing fourth supplier for IT services and grew to $100 million annual revenue (double the $50 million that was at risk originally). However, the story went further. After announcing the four preferred partners for offshore IT services, the newly merged company conducted an annual appraisal of each vendor's performance. This was measured over several headings from quality, cost, and timeliness to value-added ideas and innovation. In all, there were some 20 heads measured and weighted by the customer. This was done internally by all the user groups. The customer vendor management team then published an annual report, where each supplier could see their name and ranking but not the names of the other three suppliers. For five of the six years, HCL was rated as number one supplier; in the other year, HCL was the second. Thus, not only had we preserved our position as a preferred partner, but we had established ourselves as the preferred partner.

The first time the betting game was used was for a $200 million total IT outsourcing deal. The betting game was utilised for the outsourcing tender that was called The Flexible Business Initiative by the client. However, in discussions with the executive, it was evident that they were not aligned to the means and benefits of the project. We fed this back to the project sponsor and offered the betting game as a means of confirming the level of executive alignment and agreed-on action priorities. We also did a Proposal-on-a-Page for this customer. In essence, these two initiatives demonstrated that we had taken care to understand the real client needs and allowed ourselves to gain credibility for our bid. We were eventually shortlisted together with Accenture and Unisys, both large multinational companies, but we became the eventual winner.

For another new name sale, we developed the 'tomorrow's news today' and 'Proposal-on-a-Page', which were the features of our final board presentation. Again, we prevailed with this new customer deal that was contracted at some $150 million.

The offer of reinvesting 2% of the revenue has been very successful in retaining existing clients. Proof of Concepts (PoC) for mobile applications to embedded software and customer experience added 5% revenue as a minimum to our annual revenue. In one example, a customer worked with us to develop their own customer experience laboratory outside their own company. This was because they had experienced 'interference' from well-meaning folk in Marketing and Product Development when they tried to do it internally. By setting up in a different office, they could recruit young innovators to develop differentiated propositions.

For the other initiatives in this section, it should not be surprising that Customer Innovation Laboratory demonstrations, Customer Experience Rooms, Lunch with the Transformers, 'No PowerPoint', and the Customer Value Portal all became standard practices for every deal with new and existing clients. I firmly believe that the improvement of our win–loss ratio from 1 in 10 to better than 1 in 3 was materially influenced by the focus on becoming differentiated, innovative, and disruptive in an otherwise blandly similar competitive market. In the last full year, my team took orders totalling $1 billion, a significant milestone from less than $2 million twelve years earlier – a compound annual growth rate of 40%! My PSP had reached a pinnacle as I had added differentiated performance to presence and behavior.

Liberation summary:

- There is much you can do to improve your win–loss ratio. Lost bids are expensive in terms of time, effort, money, and goodwill.
- Verify what your win–loss ratio has been over the past two years and declare an improvement goal for the next biennium.
- Assume that all competitors can 'do the job' and that similarity in bids should be considered the norm.
- Even with the best and the brightest people, a compelling proposition, and good client interaction, you can still lose.
- Understand how to price to win. Do a forensic analysis on all the elements of the proposed solutions' costs and third parties, including margin, contingency, and risk premium.
- Build an internal case, based on the forensics, for all suitably qualified 'must-win' deals. Obtain the budget, resources, and senior management support as a pre-condition to bidding.
- Understand how the customer will evaluate bids with scoring and weighting. Keep asking, as it is in

their interests that you submit a compelling bid to secure the benefits that the customer has declared.

- For a 'must-win' bid, include a 'get well plan' on how the margin can be improved in the future.
- Always assume that a 'me too' bid will never win and incumbents will always prevail.
- Develop plans to make your bid...
  - **Differentiated**: If you know what competitors will do, do the opposite. If they will use PowerPoint, don't. If they will not accept a meeting with non-managerial delivery team members, do it.
  - **Innovative**: Think Proposal-on-a-Page, run a betting game, include a 'tomorrow's news today' article in your executive summary. Bring your own innovations, things you imagine others will not do or find difficult.
  - **Disruptive**: Include items that will hurt competition and reduce the short-term profitability of your bid. Agree to them as incentives and platform building for future additional work – same for less, cannibalising revenue and 2% reinvestment of annual revenue as a stimulus for your creativity.

Most importantly, develop your own ideas and propositions for D.I.D in your business. This will definitely impact your PSP positively.

Workshops on offer

Liberating the Manager has been written against the background of seismic changes in business. Traditional management training is increasingly struggling to keep up. Even then, management theory too frequently diverges from actual experience. Liberating the Manager is based on 100% personal experience in business from IT services, financial services, dotcom start-up and management consulting. The aim is to offer managers a guide to delivering differentiated customer value through liberation from the vast majority of fears faced by managers. Liberation from concern about being valued, liberation from the concern of having to have all the answers, liberation from constraints imposed by one's cultural heritage, liberation form worrying too much and negativity, liberation form risky hiring of people and for sales managers, liberation from losing bids too often. There are examples of methodologies that have been successful in delivering differentiated performance across different businesses. These are the subject of workshops that are offered on a direct or train-the-trainer basis. These include:

1. How to avoid risky hiring using the **Sums process**

2. How to reveal the fears and concerns preventing greater success, the **Vomit sessions**

3. How to differentiate, innovate and disrupt as a means of improving sales win ratios. **D.I.D**

4. How to improve your **Personal Share Price** (PSP) a concept introduced in the book

5. How to validate executive alignment and actions for a given strategy, the **Betting Game**.

Workshop offering: How to avoid risky hiring - The Sums process

Requirements: A manager trained in the Sums process, paper and pen to record the Sums process during an interview.

Time needed: Conducted entirely during the candidate interview.

Deliverables: A written record, completed by the candidate, of their relevant experience and ambition with respect to the most important attributes and aspects required for the role they are applying for.

From interviewing experiences and training, I developed an interview process that has served me well. What surprised me is that frequently, the interviewees remarked that they had not experienced a similar process, and had quite enjoyed it. Furthermore, when more than one of us interviewed the same person, I was able to find material evidence and candidate experience that colleagues had not picked up. When Human Resources (HR) colleagues sat in on interviews, they too commented on how the process provided relevant information in a relatively short time that gave deeper insight into candidates' skills and experience. Praise from the HR is praise indeed.

In some cases, even though the candidate had been pre-vetted by the HR, the process I developed was able to uncover facts that indicated the unsuitability of the candidate for the role in question. The technique is simple to learn and implement and greatly reduces the risk of hiring for both sides, and provides a record of each candidate's evaluation of themselves. I called this the Sums process.

The workshop can be done either as direct training to a group of managers or as a train-the-trainer model. Prior to the workshop the facilitator will need an appreciation of current methodologies used in recruitment, and any associated artefacts.

The Sums process is not intended to replace any existing systems and is additional to any prescribed or normal interview and CV evaluation. The Sums process provides an easy to use structure for candidates to reveal their experiences in a way suited to the role they are applying for. It is designed to be used by managers during an interview as a natural flow of interviewing a candidate. It provides tangible evidence of suitability by the candidate themselves, based on their past experience and performance. The innovation is that this is achieved from the candidate completing the Sums process not the interviewing manager. Thus it is a candidates self evaluation. This liberates the manager from assuming or taking complete responsibility for interpreting the candidates CV and job interview. Furthermore the process provides a written record BY THE CANDIDATE, and thus is completely objective. The written record will also provide HR with the interview summary usually requested but rarely provided! Where one or more candidates are under consideration following other interviews, the Sums process output will provide valuable means for comparison and discussion to better inform a final decision.

Contact: stuartdrew@gmail.com

Workshop offering - How to reveal the fears and concerns of a team to enable greater success - The Vomit session process

Requirements: A facilitator trained in the process, a private room, two flip charts and pens

Time needed: half a day (4-5 hours)

Deliverables: A complete record of concerns that a team is facing. A secondary session will reveal concerns regarding individual and team shortcomings. For both sessions action plans will be developed.

Whenever I inherited a new business unit, early on in my interaction with my new team, I would ask the leaders to gather with their direct reports for an unscripted planning session using a marker pen and a blank flipchart. I would introduce myself and reflect on the recent performance, good or bad, and ask the assembled team to list all the things that were preventing them from being successful or being even more successful. Invariably, the sessions started slowly. No one wanted to be the first to complain, lest they be seen as negative. Most waited for their team leaders to start. However, gradually people would pipe up with 'safe' suggestions – our pricing was high compared to the competitors, we did not invest enough on advertising, and we spent too much time on administration rather than doing our jobs. The sessions always seemed to follow a symphonic pattern – Beginning with a slow movement, building to a crescendo, then calming to a satisfying finale. I came to call these sessions – Vomit sessions, designed to get all the 'nasty's' out onto the flipchart. The vomit in fact holds the real issues that people are reluctant to volunteer for fear of reprisal

The process is offered as a workshop for a group of managers or a team and as a train-the-trainer session. The process is simple but needs to follow a prescribed pattern in order to reveal the Vomit (deeply held issues preventing further success). The Vomit represents the real issues that the team is facing and the fears of individual inadequacies. Facilitators will only be required to encourage contributions until the audience has exhausted the list of their issues preventing further success. The output is then reviewed with participants to confirm understanding. The resultant output is then classified into issues that are under the team's control, those items that they can only influence others to change and the items that are neither under the team's control or influence. From the classifications actions and owners can be agreed to deal with the issues identified as under the team's control and influence. No actions are necessary for the items neither under the team's control or influence, frequently the largest number of issues! A second session with the same team is conducted where individuals write up their own shortcomings preventing further success. This will reveal training and support needs across the team and individuals.

Contact: stuartdrew@gmail.com

Workshop offering - How to differentiate, innovate and disrupt as a means of improving sales win ratio - The D.I.D process

Requirements: A manager trained in the D.I.D process and a bid team for a **must-win** customer proposal. A note-taker needs to be in attendance to capture the workshop actions.

Time needed: An initial session of 4-6 hours. Follow up sessions during the bid process if needed. Follow up sessions will be required until bid submission..

Deliverables: Complete program of actions and deliverables for a winning proposal that is differentiated, innovative and disruptive, thus optimizing the chances of winning a competitive bid.

A 'me too' bid will never win with a new customer in the commercial world. A 'me too' bid may win with an existing customer, but with considerable future risk. Thus, it is the safest to assume that a 'me too' bid will never win in a new client situation. All bids include multiple components and moving parts. These naturally include decision makers, recommenders and influencers on the customer side. Each of these individuals has a network of colleagues, past and present, who may play a part in the bid process. In the background, consulting firms advise the board, not necessarily concerning the bid per se, but eventually their opinion is sought in the general discussion, if not formally. Also, assume that the 'golf club' syndrome is at work. Influencers, recommenders and decision makers invariably discuss their business matters with social colleagues, and they have an opinion based on recent or past experience, rumour or hearsay. The media may also play a part in articles or programmes exposing companies' successes, difficulties, practices, or scams and scandals. Industry analysts publish their supplier evaluations which may be referenced. Thus, it is safe to assume that there will be many outside influences, each of which can trip you up or enhance your bid. The point is you are never likely to know. So, what is to be done?

The workshop will examine and use any internal process for deciding a bid or no-bid decision. A list of known or likely competitors will be drawn up and a brief assessment of what they might bid with any differentiated strengths they may have for example as an incumbent supplier. A flip chart session will then be run to examine what can be included in the bid that demonstrates true differentiation from known or assumed competitors. A second and third flip chart session will identify how the proposal can prove to be truly innovative and disruptive. The last element is defined as something that may be unattractive to your bid margin but crucially something other bidders are unlikely to match or will not do (e.g. destroy existing margin for an incumbent supplier). Again there are several practical and proven examples that will be used to provoke thinking to arrive at a bid that exemplifies D.I.D principles. During the process it is assumed board level and finance approval will be required. Where the margin of the final deal is severely challenging the team will develop a Get Well plan to recover margin over the life of the contract. Regardless of a bid win or loss, the workshop will have developed valuable material for subsequent bids and wider application.

Contact: stuartdrew@gmail.com

Workshop offering - How to improve your Personal Share Price (PSP)

Requirements: A team session in a private room with flip chart and pens.

Time needed: An initial session of 4-5 hours, follow up as needed.

Deliverables: An awareness of the need to consider performance, presence and behaviour as key components for assessing one's own value to the business. An action plan will be created to establish and develop the PSP.

In thinking about how I could measure my own value in an increasingly changing world, I came up with the idea that the principal thing that mattered was what I called my Personal Share Price (PSP). This is a volatile concept, valued on a daily basis, and is not linear with regard to performance.

For example, in the corporate world, it is possible for a share price to fall against good reported performance. In July 2015, a headline in The Guardian newspaper in the UK read as follows: 'Apple stock continues to tumble despite better-than-expected earnings.' Similarly, companies can report relatively poor earnings but the share price can rise. In February 2016, Royal Dutch Shell, the global oil company, reported that its full-year earnings fell by 53%, and yet, the share price rose by 7% on the news! I do not intend to rationalise the workings of stock markets but a share price is influenced by future expectations and market sentiment, not just performance. And so, I firmly contend that the same concepts apply to individuals in assessing their contribution to work.

I contend that the Personal Share Price (PSP) has three main components, namely performance, behaviour and presence. The important principle behind PSP is that it relies on external evidence that you can collect to self validate your value to the business. Thus PSP is a self critique and valuation. In this way establishing and developing PSP is not in conflict, and is separate to, any existing company measurement system like annual appraisals

The workshop examines the concept of Personal Share Price defining what elements of external validation can be gathered to firstly establish and then develop a PSP. The implementation of 360 degree feedback will be developed on behaviour and presence (not performance) to include colleagues and external customers. An evaluation of desired behaviours to support corporate objectives will be examined or developed with actions to record compliance and improvement. Actions on how to de-personalise criticism and solicit support will be examined. Major pitfalls to achieving an improved PSP will be highlighted. Attitudes and behaviours that demonstrate openness and approachability will be discussed. Simple but effective actions will be covered including seemingly mundane things like 'thank you' notes. The appropriate use of a sense of humour will be discussed as a means of diffusing anxiety or anger. Finally appearance and posture will be discussed in a way to invite self critique. Actions to improve behaviour, presence and performance will be produced.

Contact: stuartdrew@gmail.com

Workshop offering: How to validate executive alignment for a given strategy. The Betting Game

Requirements: A manager trained in the Betting Game, Up to 10 printed sheets with the strategy statement and separate priorities supporting the strategy statement. 10 betting chips for each participant and a large table will be needed for the bets to be placed on.

Time needed: 1-2 hours per session

Deliverables: A real-time result of participant priorities based on the number of chips on each of the choices. The session includes a prioritised list of actions evidenced by the participants is a second betting round.

The betting game is very useful in checking that priorities for objectives are agreed upon and that the actions to achieve the most important objectives have executive alignment. The betting game provides a means of exploring priorities and revealing any issues with executive team alignment. There is sometimes an issue with what customers see as important and the alignment of the customer's senior management, let alone other workers, on priorities. It can be difficult, therefore, for a potential supplier of services to understand what to focus on. Speaking to different stakeholders can reveal different priorities, and at worst, divergence from the agreed board and published objectives. The challenge for a supplier is how to respond to a situation where customer executives are not agreed or aligned to an objective or means of achieving it. One innovation that worked for me was the introduction of a betting game when such situations arose. This not only brings out the issues of difference or customer alignment but does it in a non-confrontational way that is in fact fun. It also positions the services company as a most professional partner.

The workshop can be done either as direct training to a group of managers or as a train-the-trainer model. Prior to the workshop the facilitator will need to have agreed a brief statement of the issue that is being examined for executive alignment and 10 or so priorities that support the statement. Each workshop participant is given ten chips, from which they place 'bets' on a maximum of three of the ten priorities. The delegates weighting of the bet is expressed by the split of the ten chips. All ten chips on one priority makes it pre-eminent; a more balanced bet across a maximum of three traits would result in a 3,3,4 spread. However, a maximum of three bets only can be placed using all ten chips for each participant. Once each participant had placed their bets, a clear and visible pattern emerges on the collective view of priorities most likely to achieve the strategic statement. Bets are counted, and a list of priorities from most popular to the least popular identified.

This process is highly interactive and fun to do and participate in. Furthermore, it provides real-time information on group thinking that can be repeated across workshops with different participants, to provide an evidence-based, consolidated view. The published results are far more likely to be adhered to and owned, as each participant is involved and allowed to express their personal view.

Contact: stuartdrew@gmail.com

Epilogue

In this book, I have shared my thoughts and experiences on a successful career as a manager and explained how I have attempted to remain relevant during an accelerated change in business and technology. I contend that in a world of ever-increasing change, one element that can lead to differentiated and sustained performance as a manager is becoming liberated from those things that impede performance by being aware of establishing and nurturing what I have called one's Personal Share Price (PSP). The premise is that personal presence and behaviour directly impact performance. These three elements combine into a PSP that can be developed, whether it is perceived or not. I have shared my thoughts and experiences so that other managers may benefit from some or all of the ideas on a journey to superior and differentiated performance through liberation.

For me, the writing has been cathartic, and I have enjoyed relating my experiences over many years into a meaningful reference record. I have been very fortunate indeed. I have worked for and with some remarkable individuals who have guided me and encouraged me to become better than I thought I could be. Along the way, I too learnt that the vast majority of people are in fact better than they believe they are, whether in business or not. I believe it is the duty of managers to help their team members become better than they think they are.

There have been two real pleasures in recent years from a business perspective. The first was a reward from coaching- and mentoring-talented individuals to deliver extraordinary results that made my business unit consistently perform well above average. In fact, my reported business metrics were a result of their efforts. When I joined HCL with a European franchise, I met an enthusiastic ethnic Indian in the Netherlands who was told that he needed to return to India as he had been unsuccessful for too long. He drove his car after taking his shoes off, which was memorable! Through working together, he became a hugely successful businessman and learnt to drive with his shoes on! He was promoted to the post of vice president within the next five years. He matured as one of the most successful people I have worked with. Another individual I recall was a man who thought he was not a salesman. He was very good at managing the delivery of IT services, and I perceived the natural talent that he had for engaging with people. He eventually took the risk of moving to sales and triumphed, securing a $100 million deal within 18 months. There are many, many other examples where I have witnessed people rise to levels of achievement that they did not think was possible. I was merely a catalyst. No one can make someone else achieve anything. It has to come from within. The pleasurable experience for me has been shining a light into a darkened space that was otherwise frightening for people, in order to release what was innately there but hidden or suppressed.

The second pleasure is in discovering India and Indian people. I once read a very short sentence that simply said – India confounds and astounds. A truer statement has never been written. According to British Airways, my Flightpath record shows that I have visited India on 91 occasions. I have also travelled on other airlines such that I have exceeded 100 trips to India. A century in cricket, the most venerated sport in

India, is recognised as a significant achievement. I am proud of achieving my century. These trips have been on business and vacation. I have attended two Indian weddings, one spectacularly grand and the other a traditional Punjabi village affair. One interesting question to ask any Indian is how many people were at their wedding. The lowest number I have heard is 300; the largest is over 4000. So I say that an Indian wedding is the joining of two dynasties, not just two people.

I have participated in Aarthi (a Hindu ritual) at Rishikesh and stayed in the hotel part of palaces, where the Maharaja and his family still live. I have also stayed in the palace that Lord Mountbatten used when he was the Viceroy of India. I have ridden an elephant and was a victim of the worst floods in 100 years in Chennai in December 2015, where I was stuck for three days with millions of others. I have experienced Diwali in Delhi and participated, much to the locals' bewilderment, in Holi at Narendra Nagar. Indeed, I am a witness to the fact that India confounds and astounds. There are so many wonders to behold, but a special place in my heart will remain forever for India.

As previously mentioned, my experiences also include working for global companies based in UK, Europe, and USA. These have been enriching in terms of developing my cultural awareness and ways of doing business. The experience at a global consulting firm was also significant in my evolution as a seasoned professional.

I end this tale of experience as I began – with a broad smile, and wish you, the reader, as many smiles on your journey to liberation as a manager.

Acknowledgements

Thank you to all the wonderful people whom I have worked with and managed. Through good times and challenging times, your support was my continued inspiration to persevere when it might have been easier to concede or give up on pursuing differentiated performance. Ideas and suggestions from my team leaders have always been welcome, especially at times when their input caused me to rethink the way forward. Together we were stronger, as you seized the empowerment offered as soon as you understood it carried no threat! I have enjoyed working with you and many clients who have enriched my experiences and caused me to smile a great deal. In particular I would like to thank Renee Platfoot who supported me for many years and took my handwritten draft of this book and made it readable.

Vineet Nayar was the most effective and charismatic leader I have worked with. His leadership for the Employee First Customer Second (EFCS) transformation of HCL was groundbreaking and global in its impact. Vineet demonstrated that a singular passion can indeed transform a global business.

Anand Pillai has been instrumental in the transformation of businesses. He and I worked together on a number of road shows and international platforms evangelising the reality of business transformation. Anand is now the managing director of his own business, aptly called Leadership Matters Inc.

Julian Birkinshaw, Professor of Strategy and Entrepreneurship, Deputy Dean Programmes, Director of the Institute of Innovation and Entrepreneurship, London Business School. Julian provided me with valuable recommendations on the structure of the book and its relevance to current management strategy.

Patti Stevens, had a similar passion many years ago for establishing a professional platform for executive coaching. This was achieved through APECS (Association for Professional Executive Coaching & Supervision), which she founded. We have shared ideas over many years about the importance of professional coaching in management.

Aniruddho Mukherjee has helped me a great deal with connections to academics and business people to validate the relevance and efficacy of this book.

None of us can give the best of our work without support from home. My wife, Alice, and children, Erin and Ashleigh, have been a constant foundation from whom I could obtain advice, encouragement, and support. They have not been afraid to tell me when I am wrong. As someone once said, no man is a hero in his own home!

My father fled from Poland during the second world war after he suffered as a prisoner of war in a Russian camp. He met my mother in the UK and they married. My brother Robert and me would sometimes reflect on the extraordinary circumstances that led to our being. Robert, himself a successful businessman, has always encouraged me, and together we owe everything that we have achieved to our parents.

Finally, thank you to all who have looked into this book and its contents, and I wish you well with your liberation journey.

Index

360 degree feedback, 14,15,16,188

A

Aarthi, 193

Alison Beard, 27

Annual appraisal, 1,6,9,176

Apple, 9,187

Atom Bank, 8

B

Betting game, 159-189

Blueprint meeting, 37

Brexit, 63

Bridge of Spies (movie), 92,96,106

C

Cannabalising revenue, 171-173

Carlos Ghosn CEO Renault-Nissan, 66

Cecil Rhodes, 66

Cultural difference, 3,51-60,120

Customer Experience Room, 155,177

Customer Value Portal, 42-44,154,177

Millennial generation, 47,62

MIT, 27

Monday Call, 82,134,136

Mr Turnbull headmaster, 24

N

Nancy Kline, 102

No PowerPoint, 153-155

P

Personal Share Price (PSP), 1,2,9-33

Proposal on a Page, 157-159

Prudential Corporation, 22,52

Q

Queen Elizabeth II, 26

R

Reinvest 2% of revenue, 173-175

Richard D. Lewis co-author, Fish Can't See Water, 66

Ricky Gervais, 110

Rishikesh, 193

Robert Half International survey, 27

Robin Stuart-Kotze, Professor, 123

Roman Catholic Cardinal Newman, 17

U

Uber, 8,11

Unisys, 3,10,19,78,141

Value creators, 39-43, 152,154

Value zone, 38,151

Vineet Nayar, 31,36,37,44,64,77

Vomit sessions, 87

W

Walter Mischel, professor, 13,123

Win–Loss ratio, 139,177

Wharton Business School, 27

'What has to be true', 57-58,63

World Economic Forum, 71,168

Y

Y generation, 47

Printed in Great Britain
by Amazon

66290682R00119